Journal of the

INDIAN WARS

Volume One, No. 1

Savas Publishing Company

202 First Street SE, Suite 103A, Mason City, IA 50401

Subscription and Publishing Information

Journal of the Indian Wars (*JIW*) is published quarterly by Savas Publishing Company, 202 First Street SE, Suite 103A, Mason City, IA 50401. Publisher: Theodore P. Savas. (515) 421-7135 (voice); (515)-421-8370 (fax); e-mail: cwbooks@mach3ww.com. Our on-line military history catalog of original books is found at www.savaspublishing.com.

SUBSCRIPTIONS to *JIW* are available at $29.95/yr. (four books); Canada and overseas is $39.95/yr. Write to: Savas Publishing Company, *JIW* Subscriptions, 202 First Street SE, Suite 103A, Mason City, IA 50401. Check, MO, MC or V accepted. Phone, fax or E-mail orders welcome. All subscriptions begin with the current issue unless otherwise specified.

DISTRIBUTION in North America is handled by Peter Rossi at Stackpole Books, 5067 Ritter Road, Mechanicsburg, PA 17055-6921. 800-732-3669 (voice); 717-976-0412 (fax); e-mail: prossi@stackpolesales.com. European distribution is through Greenhill Books, Park House, 1 Russell Gardens, London NW11 9NN, England; e-mail: LionelLeventhal@compuserve.com; Back issues of *JIW* are available through Stackpole Books or your local bookseller. Retail price is $11.95 plus shipping ($4.00 for the first book and $1.00 for each additional book). Check, money order, MC/V, AE, or D are accepted. Contact Stackpole Books for quantity discounts.

MANUSCRIPTS, REVIEWS, AND NEWS SUBMISSIONS are welcome. For author or reviewer guidelines, please consult our web site (www.savaspublishing.com) or send a self-addressed stamped envelope to Michael A. Hughes, Managing Editor, *Journal of the Indian Wars*, 834 East Sixth Street, Box E, Ada, OK 74820. Proposals for articles (recommended) should include a brief description of your topic, a list of primary sources, and a conservative estimate of the completion date. Manuscripts will not be returned without proper postage. Persons interested in reviewing books should send a description of their qualifications, areas of expertise, and desired titles and topics. News submissions should include a brief abstracted version of any information. Submitted news may be posted on our web site at our discretion. Enclose a SASE if requesting a reply to any correspondence and include your E-mail and fax number. Publications (which may include page proofs) and videos for potential review should be sent to the managing editor.

JIW is published with the cooperation of Jerry Russell and the Order of the Indian Wars. Without Jerry's non-too-gentle proddings and earnest supplications, it would not have come to fruition. For more information on the OIW, please write to P.O. Box 3559, Little Rock AR.

Savas Publishing Company

Publisher
Theodore P. Savas

Editorial
Dana Shoaf
William Haley

Graphics
Monalisa DiAngelo

Cartography
Mark A. Moore

Marketing
Nancy Lund

Indexing
Lee W. Merideth

Journal of the Indian Wars

Editor
Michael A. Hughes

Editorial Consultants
Brian Pohanka, Jerry Keenan,
Neil Mangum, Jerry Russell,
and Ted Alexander

Advertising/Circulation
Nancy Lund
Carol A. Savas

Associate Editors: Patrick Bowmaster and Eril B. Hughes

Civil War Regiments Journal

Managing Editor
Mark A. Snell

Assistant Editor
Mark Bell

Circulation
Carol A. Savas

Advertising
Nancy Lund

Book Review Editor
Archie McDonald

Desktop Publishing
Albert Pejack, Jr.

Contributors

Neil C. Mangum is the new superintendent of the Little Bighorn Battlefield National Monument. Mangum is regarded as an authority on the Sioux War of 1876-1877, having formerly been a historian at the Little Bighorn battlefield for nine years and author of an important book on the Battle of the Rosebud. He was also involved in locating and describing a wide range of battlefields while conducting documentary and archaeological investigation for the National Battlefield Protection Program. The editors of *JIW* would like to thank Neil for taking the time to contribute to this issue and join many others in wishing Neil a long and rewarding tenure at the park.

Bob Rea is the supervisor of the Fort Supply Historic Site. He has worked in the documentation and archaeological surveys of the Washita Battlefield National Historic Site and Camp Supply, and has written articles and reports on a number of western Oklahoma battlefields.

C. Lee Noyes is a trade supervisor with the U.S. Bureau of Customs in New York State. He produces several speeches and articles each year on Plains warfare, particularly on the Little Bighorn Campaign.

William B. Lees is the administrator of the historical sites of the Oklahoma Historical Society and an archaeologist. In addition to the Washita Battlefield dig, he was also part of the team that excavated the Mine Creek, KS, Civil War battlefield (1874), as well as another team that concluded that the location of the 1874 Sand Creek Massacre remains in serious doubt.

Sarah L. Craighead, the new superintendent at Washita Battlefield, is a veteran of the National Park Service. She first worked at Mammoth Cave, and then at five other parks, including Manassas NBP. She was most recently assistant chief of interpretation at Mesa Verde National Park. The editors of *JIW* thank Sarah for her article and her role in rapidly increasing public interpretation and access at Washita.

Rodney G. Thomas is a professional army officer whose career has spanned three decades, 19 countries, and survival of one tour in the Pentagon. Rod, who will retire this year, operates a business consulting firm, Pacific Paladin, Inc., in Hawaii and is the webmaster for the 3rd Armored Division web site (www.3ad.com). He belongs to a number of organizations, including the Little Bighorn Association and The Order of the Indian Wars. In addition to contributing biographical entries on Native American women warriors for a book by Greenwood Press, Rod has his own book on Indian art and the Battle of the Little Bighorn coming soon from Upton & Sons.

Journal of the INDIAN WARS

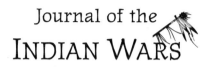

Table of Contents

continued

Table of Contents (continued)

This month's cover artwork is "Attack at Dawn," by Charles Schreyvogel,
courtesy of the Gilcrease Museum, Tulsa, Oklahoma.

Editor's Foreword

Welcome to the inaugural issue of *Journal of the Indian Wars* (*JIW*) a periodical which marks the beginning of a novel publishing venture. *JIW* is unique in its exclusive focus—the American Indian wars. As historian Neil Mangum cogently observes in his Introduction, fountains of ink have been expended in describing the American Civil War, while the Indian wars have remained largely obscure. *JIW* proudly sets forth in an attempt to remedy that oversight.

At the same time, *JIW* will be unique in its breadth and depth. In addition to general histories, we will offer insightful articles and interviews on the strategies, tactics, technology, art, weaponry, policies, and consequences of almost three hundreds years of continental conflicts. While the majority of our articles will focus on warfare in the West from 1848 to 1890, *JIW* will not ignore the fascinating Indian wars history east of the Mississippi River. Equally important, *JIW* will publish original articles that meet high scholarly standards *and* that can be understood and appreciated by general readers as well as long-standing students of the conflicts. *JIW* also seeks to develop a new interest in the Indian Wars.

Volume One, No. 1 examines George A. Custer's two most famous Indian battles: Washita (1868) and Little Bighorn (1876). The coverage is anything but conventional, and a glance at the table of contents reveals the variety of subjects and approaches that readers will come to expect from *JIW*.

Bob Rea and C. Lee Noyes open this issue with traditional articles, the former dealing with logistical issues, and the latter with strategic comparisons and observations. Their work is expanded and enhanced by a pair of articles which follow, the first by William B. Lees and the second by Sarah Craighead. Dr. Lees' essay, the first published account of excavations at Washita Battlefield, reminds us once again that archaeological discoveries complement written records. The scene of Black Kettle's demise is now Washita Battlefield National Historic Site, and as its superintendent, Craighead writes of the growing concern for including Native Indian perspectives in writing Indian wars' history. In stark contrast to more traditional approaches to history is Rodney G. Thomas' article on "Kicking Bear's Canvas," which shows how Indian art is a valuable historical resource for understanding the past. Another "specialized" treatment entails the presentation of a special section of ledgerbook artwork produced by Cheyenne Dog Soldiers, which lets readers draw some of their own conclusions about Plain Indian warfare.

Many individuals and institutions have been particularly generous with their time and resources in the preparation of this issue. Particular thanks are due to superintendents Neil Mangum and Sarah Craighead of the National Park Service, Dr. Lees and Bob Rea of the Oklahoma Historical Society, the Colorado Historical Society and the Gilcrease Museum, and above all to the two who first envisioned the journal, Jerry L. Russell of the Order of the Indian Wars, and the publisher, Theodore P. Savas.

Michael A. Hughes
Editor

Differing Approaches

The Battles of the Washita
and Little Bighorn

*T*he following summaries of the Battles of the Washita (1868) and the Little Bighorn (1876) are included in this issue for two reasons. First, they provide a general framework for better understanding and appreciating the wide variety of articles contained in this issue. Second, the two summaries are included as representations of different periods and approaches in the writing of history. The latter summary, detailing the battle of the Little Bighorn, was written by the Center of Military History, United States Army. It was printed in 1969 and revised in 1973 and 1989, but borrows heavily from a 1956 text. The army's account is traditional military history and represents an era when military, political, and economic history were dominant. The first summary, on the Battle of the Washita, was produced in 1998 by the National Park Service for the visitors to the new Washita Battlefield National Historic Site in Oklahoma. The Washita account is partially based on a 1976 military history by Stan Hoig. The Park Service's text, however, evidences the current tendency to emphasize the social and cultural causes and consequences of events.

*   *   *

"The Story of the Battle of the Washita"
The National Park Service

Introduction

The cultural collision between pioneers and Indians reached its peak on the Great Plains during the decades before and after the Civil War. U.S. Government policy sought to separate tribes and settlers from each other by establishing an Indian Territory (present-day Oklahoma). Some Plains tribes accepted life on reservations. Others, including the Cheyenne, Kiowa, and

Commanche, did not. They continued to hunt and live on traditional lands outside the Indian Territory At first, this choice produced little conflict. But following the Civil War, land-hungry settlers began penetrating the plains in increasing numbers, encroaching upon tribal hunting grounds. Indians could no longer retreat beyond the reach of whites, and many chose to defend their freedom and lands rather than submit to reservation life.

Prelude to Battle

Events leading to the Battle of the Washita began with the Sand Creek Massacre of 1864. On November 29, 1864, troops under the command of Col. J. M. Chivington attacked and destroyed the Cheyenne camp of Chief Black Kettle and Chief White Antelope on Sand Creek, 40 miles from Fort Lyon, Colorado Territory. Black Kettle's band flew an American flag and a white flag, and considered themselves at peace and under military protection. The terrible slaughter caused a massive public outcry. In response, a Federal Peace Commission was created to convert Plains Indians from their nomadic way of life and settle them on reservations.

On the Southern Plains, the work of the Commission culminated in the Medicine Lodge Treaty of October 1867. Under treaty terms the Arapahos, Cheyenne, Comanches, Kiowas, and Plains Apaches were assigned to reservations in the Indian Territory. There they were supposed to receive permanent homes, farms, agricultural implements, and annuities of food, blankets, and clothing. The treaty was doomed to failure. Many tribal officials refused to sign. Some who did sign had no authority to compel their people to comply with such an agreement. War parties, mostly young men violently opposed to reservation life, continued to raid white settlements in Kansas.

Major General Philip H. Sheridan, in command of the Department of Missouri, adopted a policy that "punishment must follow crime." In retaliation for the Kansas raids, he planned to mount a winter campaign when Indian horses would be weak and unfit for everything but the most limited service. The Indians' only protection in winter was the isolation afforded by brutal weather.

Black Kettle and Arapaho Chief Big Mouth went to Fort Cobb in November 1868 to petition Gen. William B. Hazen for peace and protection. A respected leader of the Southern Cheyenne, Black Kettle had signed the Little Arkansas Treaty in 1865 and the Medicine Lodge Treaty in 1867. After giving

Washita Battlefield. These are the only monuments on the battlefield, as they appear from a viewing pavilion. The inscribed monument was placed by the Oklahoma Historical Society prior to the battlefield's recent entry into the National Park system. The high ground in the field beyond the fence was used for a skirmish line by Custer's troops. The appearance on the distant high ground of Arapaho warriors from a nearby village was a factor in Custer's decision to withdraw and leave Maj. Joel Elliott's detachment behind. *Michael A. Hughes*

the two chiefs flour, blankets, and other goods, Hazen told them that he could not allow them to bring their people to Fort Cobb for protection because only General Sheridan or Lt. Col. George Custer, his field commander, had that authority. Disappointed, the chiefs headed back to their people at the winter encampments on the Washita River.

The Battle of the Washita

Even as Black Kettle and Big Mouth parlayed with General Hazen, the Seventh Cavalry established a forward base of operations at Camp Supply, Indian Territory, as part of Sheridan's winter campaign strategy. Under orders from Sheridan, Custer marched south on November 23 with about 800 troopers, traveling through a foot of new snow. After four days of travel, the command reached the Washita Valley shortly after midnight on November 27, and silently took up a position near an Indian encampment their scouts had discovered at a bend in the river.

Black Kettle, who had just returned from Fort Cobb a few days before, had resisted the entreaties of some of his people, including his wife, to move their camp downriver closer to larger encampments of Cheyenne, Kiowas, and Apaches wintered there. He refused to believe that Sheridan would order an attack without first offering an opportunity for peace.

Before dawn, the troopers attacked the 51 lodges, killing a number of men, women, and children. Custer reported about 100 killed, though Indian accounts claimed 11 warriors plus 19 women and children. Custer's losses were light: two officers and 19 enlisted men killed. Most of the soldier casualties belonged to Maj. Joel Elliott's detachment, whose eastward foray was overrun by Cheyenne, Arapaho, and Kiowa warriors coming to Black Kettle's aid. Chief Black Kettle and his wife were killed in the attack.

Following Sheridan's plan to cripple resistance, Custer ordered the slaughter of the Indian pony and mule herd estimated at more than 800 animals. The lodges of Black Kettle's people, with all their winter supply of food and clothing, were torched. Realizing now that many more Indians were threatening from the east, Custer feigned an attack toward their downriver camps, then quickly retreated to Camp Supply with his hostages.

The engagement at the Washita might have ended very differently if the larger encampments to the east had been closer to Black Kettle's camp. As it happened, the impact of losing winter supplies, plus the knowledge that cold weather no longer provided protection from attack, convinced many bands to accept reservation life.

Washita Battlefield. Three of this issue's authors, Bob Rea, William B. Lees (center), and Sarah Craighead, are shown standing on the only U.S. troop position currently excavated on the battlefield. Black Kettle's village was located in the bottom lands of the Washita River seen behind Lees' shoulder. George Custer may have crossed a bend of the river to enter the Cheyenne village in the tree line seen behind Dr. Lees' head. *Michael A. Hughes*

"The Northern Plains"

Center of Military History, United States Army

All of the elements of the clash of red and white civilization were present in the events leading to final subjugation of the Indians. The mounted tribes of the Great Plains were astride the main corridors of westward expansion, and this was the area of decision. The treaty of 1868 had set aside the Great Sioux Reservation in South Dakota and the Army had abandoned the Bozeman Trail, leaving the Powder River region as unceded Indian country. The Sioux and their allies were thus north of the main transcontinental artery along the Platte. Although the arrangement worked for several years, it was doomed by the irresistible march of civilization. The Sioux rejected white overtures for a right-of-way for the Northern Pacific Railroad, and when surveyors went ahead anyway they ran into Indian resistance, which led to the dispatch in 1873 of a large military expedition under Col. David S. Stanley up the Yellowstone Valley. The next year General Sheridan sent Custer and the Seventh Cavalry on a reconnaissance through the Black Hills, within the Sioux Reservation. When geologists with the expedition found gold, the word spread rapidly and prospectors filtered into the area despite the Army's best efforts to keep them out. Another treaty was broken and, band by band, angry reservation Indians slipped away to join non-treaty recalcitrants in the unceded Powder River region of Wyoming and Montana.

In December 1875 the Indian bureau notified the Sioux and Cheyenne that they had to return to the reservation by the end of the following month. Since the Indians were in winter quarters in remote areas and would have had little chance against the elements, they did not obey. As the deadline passed, the Commissioner of Indian Affairs appealed to the Army to force compliance. Sheridan, mindful of the success with converging columns against the Southern Plains tribes, determined upon a similar campaign in the north.

Columns were organized to move on the Powder River area from three directions. Brigadier General Alfred H. Terry marched westward from Fort Abraham Lincoln in Dakota Territory, his principal element the Seventh cavalry under George Custer. Colonel John Gibbon moved eastward from Fort Ellis in western Montana with a mixed forced of infantry and cavalry, while Brig. Gen. George Crook moved northward from Fort Fetterman on the North Platte in Wyoming with a force heavily weighted in cavalry.

In March 1876 a part of Crook's force under Col. Joseph J. Reynolds entered the valley of the Powder and surprised a Cheyenne-Sioux camp, but Reynolds failed to press an initial advantage and withdrew without punishing the Indians. In June, with the major campaign under way, Crook made the first contact. The Sioux and Cheyenne learned of his approach along Rosebud Creek, and some 1,500 warriors moved to meet him. Crook had fifteen companies of cavalry and five of infantry, about 1,000 men, plus another 300 friendly Indians and civilians. The two forces met on roughly equal terms on June 17 in heavy fighting. Tactically, neither side carried the field conclusively enough to claim a victory. Strategically, Crook's withdrawal to a supply base to southward gave the Battle of the Rosebud the complexion of a defeat for the Army, especially in view of developments on the Little Bighorn River about fifty miles to northwestward, which his continued advance might have influenced decisively.

While Crook was moving northward to his collision on the Rosebud, Terry and Gibbon, marching from east and west, had joined forces on the Yellowstone River at its confluence with the Powder, where a supply base serviced by river steamer was established. Terry sent out the Seventh Cavalry to scout for Indians, and Maj. Marcus A. Reno with six companies (the cavalry "company" was not called a "troop" until 1883) reconnoitered up the Powder, across the Tongue River, and into the valley of the Rosebud. There, on June 17, Reno found a fresh trail leading west out of the valley and across the Wolf Mountains in the direction of the Little Bighorn. He was unaware, and was thus unable to inform his superiors, that Crook was also in the Rosebud Valley and had been engaged and blocked by a large force of Indians not far upstream on that very same day.

Terry held a council of war aboard the steamboat *Far West* to outline his plan. Custer's Seventh Cavalry would move south up the Rosebud, cross the Wolf Mountains, and enter the Little Bighorn Valley from the south. Gibbon, joined by Terry, would ascend the Bighorn River and its tributary, the Little Bighorn, from the north, trapping the Indians between the two forces.

As it happened, Custer moved at least a day early for the cooperative action envisioned in Terry's plan. On June 25, 1876, the Seventh crossed the Wolf Mountains and moved into the valley of the Little Bighorn. Custer was confident of his ability to handle whatever he ran up against, convinced that the Indians would follow their usual practice of scattering before a show of force.

Little Bighorn Battlefield. The Deep Ravine drains into the Little Bighorn River (barely visible between the trees) from the southwestern slope of the ridge along which fell the five companies of George Custer's detachment. In the 1980s, archaeological exploration under the direction of Douglas D. Scott and Richard A. Fox, Jr., turned up some of the last unmarked human remains on the battlefield in this ravine. *C. Lee Noyes*

Custer was completely unaware that he was descending upon one of the largest concentrations of Indians ever assembled on the Plains—perhaps as many as 12,000 to 15,000 Sioux and Northern Cheyenne, with between 3,000 and 4,000 warriors under such leaders as Crazy Horse, Sitting Bull, Gall, Crow King, Lame Deer, Hump, and Two Moon.

Around noon of this Sunday in June, Custer sent Capt. Frederick W. Benteen with three companies to scout to the left of the command, not an unusual move for a force still attempting to fix the location of an elusive enemy and expecting him to slip away on contact. About 2:30 p.m., still two miles short of the river, when the upper end of an Indian village came into view, Custer advanced three more companies under Major Reno with instructions to cross the river and charge the Indian camp. With five companies Custer moved off to the right, still screened by a fold of ground from observing the extent of his opposition, perhaps with the thought of hitting the Indians from the flank—of letting Reno hold the enemy by the nose while he, Custer, kicked him in the seat of the pants. As he progressed, Custer rushed Sgt. Daniel Kanipe to the rear to hurry the pack train and its one-company escort forward, and shortly afterward dispatched Trumpeter John Martin with a last message to Benteen informing him that a "big village" lay ahead and to "be quick—bring packs."

The main phase of the Battle of the Little Bighorn lasted about two hours. Reno, charging down the river with three companies and some Arickara scouts, ran into hordes of Indians, not retreating, but advancing, perhaps mindful of their creditable performance against Crook a week before, and certainly motivated by a desire to protect their women and children and cover a withdrawal of the villages. Far outnumbered, suffering heavy casualties, and in danger of being overrun, Reno withdrew his command to the bluffs across the river and dug in.

Custer and his five companies—about 230 strong—moved briskly along the bluffs of the river until, some four miles away, beyond supporting distance and out of sight of the rest of the command, they were brought to bay and overwhelmed by an Indian force that outnumbered them by perhaps 20 to 1. When the last man had fallen and the dead had been plundered, the Indians turned their attention to Reno once again.

While the Indians had been chiefly absorbed on the Custer section of the field, Benteen's battalion and the pack train and its escorting company had moved up and gone into a defensive perimeter with Reno's force. An attempt to move in force in Custer's direction, despite a complete lack of knowledge of his location and situation, failed; the Reno defensive position was reoccupied and remained under attack until dark of the 25th and on through daylight hours of the 26th. The siege was finally lifted with the arrival of the Terry-Gibbon column on June 27.

The Custer disaster shocked the nation and was the climax of the Indian wars. The Army poured troops into the Upper Plains and the Indians scattered, some, like Sitting Bull's band, to Canada. Gradually, under Army pressure or seeing the futility of further resistance, the Indians surrendered and returned to the reservation.

*   *   *

Introduction

The Needs of Indian Wars History

Neil C. Mangum

I am pleased to have a part in the premier issue of *Journal of the Indian Wars*, a scholarly and popular magazine devoted to the study and understanding of the Indian wars on the North American frontier. With the exception of noted park battlefields such as Little Bighorn or military posts such as Fort Laramie and Fort Davis, the Indian wars have been forgotten or ignored by a large segment of the continent's population. Hopefully, with the creation of this journal, that will change.

Compared to the amount of ink spilled on the study of American Civil War events, the Indian wars receive hardly a drop. Unfortunately, most of what has been written on the subject is a saturation and fascination with a few selected themes, such as the 1876-1877 "Sioux War" or the Geronimo Campaign (1881-1886). Other notable events, such as the Red River War (1874-1875) and the Victorio Campaign (1877-1880) go almost unheralded. I urge historians and interested writers to expand their horizons beyond the publicized sites to research and publish on other equally significant but lesser known events.

Chronicling the Indian wars will be challenging, for if it is to be good history, honest history, it must be inclusive of the perspective of all cultures. Most of the standard works on the Indian wars were written in an era when the viewpoint was that of the conquerors. Histories of the Indian wars have often omitted Indian accounts. As seen by the recent shift in writings and interpretations at Little Bighorn Battlefield, the Indian point of view is now emerging as an integral component of the story of the battle in that park. Indian oral histories, once rejected by Indian wars historians because less value was placed on the spoken word than the written word, are now finally winning acceptance as an excellent source of historical information.

The type of transformation evidenced at Little Bighorn must continue in presenting the story of other subjects related to the Indian wars. These changes should incorporate new research and new themes, including the perspective of women (that of both Indians and Army dependents), the role of civilian employees, and the economic impact of the military presence on local communities.

The study of the Indian wars faces other challenges beyond that of wider cultural inclusion. Most Indian wars battlefields do not benefit from any type of permanent protection. Many sites have been destroyed by the less responsible sort of land developers and relic hunters. Some battlefields have never been located due to their remoteness or the dearth of information about an event. Historians should not be satisfied with merely writing good history—they must be advocates for the historic preservation of all Indian wars sites. It is not enough to only write about the Indian wars: we must strive to preserve and protect the physical evidence of our heritage. There are hundreds of Indian wars sites waiting to be discovered.

This collection of articles and columns is a great start down this path. It is my hope and desire that in succeeding issues of *Journal of the Indian Wars*, articles will appear that address some of the concerns outlined above.

Sheridan & Custer

Camp Supply and the Winter Campaign of 1868-1869

Bob Rea

For several miles, a tongue of bottomland divides Wolf Creek and Beaver River before they join to form the North Canadian River of present day Oklahoma. Into this valley in late 1868 came the largest military expedition yet assembled on the Southern Plains. Its mission was to carry out a bold new plan, a campaign to attack the winter encampments of the Cheyenne, Arapaho, Kiowa, and Comanche nations. A "camp of supply" to support a striking force consisting of eleven companies of the Seventh U.S. Cavalry Regiment and ten of the Nineteenth Kansas Volunteer Cavalry Regiment was now being established under Field Order No. 8, dated November 19, 1868. The camp was established under Lt. Col. Alfred Sully, who was in nominal command of the campaign.

Across the plain and along the tree lined banks was a canvas city with rows of infantry "A" tents, cavalry canvas shelter halves, wall tents, and over 400 wagons. Soldiers and teamsters were immediately put to work felling trees, mowing hay, unloading supplies. These men were preparing for what promised to be a grueling winter expedition in virtually unknown country against an unconventional foe. The campaign's author, Lt. Gen. Philip Sheridan, commanding the Division of the Missouri, rode into camp on November 20 to personally oversee the planned offensive.

A stockade was built in this wilderness for the protection of the infantry and for use as an ammunition magazine. The ten-foot high walls enclosed two long storehouses. Two blockhouses sat at opposite corners, while half-dugouts formed lunettes (crescent-shaped earthworks) at the other two angles. A collection of crude huts resembling the winter quarters of the armies of the

American Civil War were thrown up for those who would be more permanent inhabitants.

The supplies for the Nineteenth

Philip Sheridan
Generals in Blue

Kansas Regiment were stored safely in the warehouses of Camp Supply well before the arrival of its men. The Kansans had become lost and besieged by snowfall to the point of starvation. Yet by the time their marching column straggled into camp, Sheridan's main strike force was in the saddle and gone. The impetuous Lt. Col. George Custer, Sheridan's subordinate, had received permission to escape the confines of the blizzard-stricken encampment. Custer's assignment was to search out and punish those Indians considered hostile for their part in raids in Kansas during the preceding warm seasons. Beyond chastising such bands, Sheridan's campaign was also meant to show all of the tribes that the Federal government meant to force them to accept the provisions of the 1867 Medicine Lodge (Kansas) Treaty.

Some seventy-five miles (120 km.) south of the supply camp, on the Washita River, Custer and his Seventh Cavalry fell on the encampment of the luckless Cheyenne chief Black Kettle (Moketaveto) on November 27, 1868. The Battle of Washita changed the course of Cheyenne and Southern Plains Indian history. The success of the winter campaign led to the implementation of such campaigns in the future against other tribes throughout the West.

A second phase of Sheridan's campaign was intended to follow up Custer's initial success. On December 7, Sheridan and Custer rolled out of Camp Supply at the head of 1,600 men and 300 wagons and pushed south to the site of the Washita battle. This time the Nineteenth Kansas accompanied the Seventh U.S. Cavalry. By the time the expedition reached its eventual destination at old Fort Cobb (1859) on December 18, the men had suffered considerably from the winter elements. But the strength and resolve demonstrated by the Army's willingness to conduct a winter pursuit convinced the Kiowa and Comanche to present themselves at a new post to the south, Fort Sill (1869) in the Wichita Mountains. The two cavalry regiments then rode west to the eastern edge of the Texas Staked Plains to bring in those Cheyenne who were still "out." By mid-March, Custer coerced these remaining Cheyenne to accept location around the new Indian Agency at Camp Supply. On March 30, Custer and the Seventh Cavalry left Camp Supply for the last time, bound for Kansas and the long trail to his death at the Little Bighorn in 1876.

The success of Sheridan and Custer's 1868-1869 winter campaign placed new importance on the frontier outpost of Camp Supply, which became a bastion of U.S. government presence and white civilization. During the campaign, Camp Supply served as the midpoint of a busy new supply trail between the military posts of Fort Dodge (Kansas) and Fort Cobb.

The "temporary" base of supply continued to survive and grow over the next twenty-four years, its role evolving with the changing frontier. Until May 1870, it served as the Cheyenne and Arapaho Indian Agency. Supplies once again flowed through the post for the Miles Expedition during the Red River War of 1874-1875. For much of its early period, its troops were kept busy protecting the Cheyenne and Arapaho from such perils as livestock thieves, whiskey peddlers, cattlemen, and land-hungry settler intruding into their reservation. The soldiers of Fort Supply were the peace keepers regulating the last "invasion" of Indian Territory (modern Oklahoma) when the region was ultimately opened to white settlement. An era in American history passed with the closing of the frontier and, in the fall of 1894, the closing of Fort Supply as well.

Today, evidence of the region's history is preserved by the Oklahoma Historical Society at the Fort Supply Historic Site. A replica of the 1868 stockade recalls the time when Sheridan and Custer camped in the valley of the streams. Five original structures evoke the memory of life in the frontier U.S. Army in the late nineteenth century. Two housing quarters of pickets (vertical logs), those used by the Ordnance Sergeant (1874) and a civilian employee of the Quartermaster (early 1880s) are rare surviving examples of a once common type of post buildings. On "Officer's Row" are located the frame Commanding Officer's Quarters (1878) and the duplex Officer's Quarters (1882). The only brick building constructed at the post is the Guardhouse (1892), which also survives. These historic structures are complemented by a visitor center building containing artifacts found on the grounds of the old post.

Although few people today know and appreciate the important logistical role played by the small supply camp, its implementation led directly to the Washita engagement and altered forever the course of Cheyenne and Southern Plains Indian history.

A Tale of Two Battles

George Armstrong Custer and the Attacks at the Washita and Little Bighorn

C. Lee Noyes

Scholars have been in heated disagreement for more than 120 years over the character and competency of George A. Custer. However convincing any article on Custer may seem, prudent editors still precede such work with the standard disclaimer that "the views expressed in this material are the author's own and do not necessarily reflect the opinions of the editors." This publication will carry on that glorious and timorous tradition. Another controversy is the ongoing argument as to whether the action at the Washita River was a "battle" or a "massacre." It should be noted that there is no evidence to suggest that Custer and his troopers set out to take the lives of non-combatants; the village harbored and was near bands of hostile Cheyenne and Arapaho. However, Black Kettle was, as author C. Lee Noyes notes, a "peace chief," and Custer's tactics at the Washita, no matter what his intent, put many women and children under fire. On one point, at least, there is no disagreement—the event at the Washita was a tragedy.

The essayist Montaigne once observed that many men's lives outlast their celebrity. If true, George Armstrong Custer is a notable exception. Custer's notoriety, both positive and negative, has continued to grow since his death in battle on the banks of the Little Bighorn River in 1876. Yet Custer's defenders and critics alike have often based their conclusions on only one phase or battle of Custer's life. Custer's allies have tended to place much of their emphasis on his Civil War career. His detractors usually concentrate on the

fatal outcome of his final battle. Curiously, both sides have often

George Armstrong Custer

Generals in Blue

ignored Custer's action on the Washita River in 1868.

As Custer led troops in only two major "battles" of the Indian wars, it is impossible to make a fair evaluation of his career on the frontier without taking both actions into account. In addition, Custer's decisions at the Little Bighorn in 1876 cannot be understood without examining the results of his earlier battle.

Known as the "Boy General" of the Civil War, Custer was promoted to that rank in 1863 while only twenty-three years of age. By war's end he had earned the stars of a major general of volunteers and had won the accolades of his superiors. One of these superiors, Gen. Philip H. Sheridan, played an important role in Custer's career from 1864 until Custer's death in 1876. Their close professional relationship was symbolized by a gift that Sheridan presented to Custer's wife the day after the surrender of the Confederate Army of Northern Virginia in 1865. To Mrs. Custer, Sheridan presented the table on which General Grant had written the conditions of surrender. "Permit me to say, Madam," he wrote in explanation, "that there is scarcely an individual in our service who contributed more to bring this [surrender] about than your very gallant husband."[1] Custer's reputation as a military hero seemed secure.

Based on his wartime record, in 1866 Custer was appointed lieutenant colonel of the newly-formed U.S. Seventh Cavalry Regiment. His "demotion" stemmed from the fact that his higher wartime ranks had been brevet appointments, ranks held temporarily while handling greater than routine responsibility. Custer exercised command of the Seventh Cavalry on and off for most of the next ten years and was the unit's dominant personality.[2]

Despite Custer's acknowledged bravery, his forceful personality and what some regarded as arbitrary decision making aroused partisan emotions during the late war. Opinions about Custer became even sharper in the next decade. Captain Albert Barnitz, for example, attributed the high desertion rate in the Seventh Cavalry during the regiment's first year to Custer's personality and reputation as a martinet. "He is the most complete example of a petty tyrant that I have ever seen," Barnitz revealed to his wife in 1867. Expressing his disgust about this perceived behavior, the captain feared the organizational and personal consequences if "Custer remains long in command. . . ."[3]

Custer's most outspoken critic, however, was the man who would be his senior company commander at the Battle of the Little Bighorn, Capt. Frederick William Benteen. Benteen later claimed that he had formed a negative opinion of the commander of the Seventh Cavalry from the very beginning. "I'm only too proud to say that I despised him as a murderer, thief and a liar," stated Benteen after Custer's death. As far as Benteen was concerned, Custer—far from demonstrating greatness—was a man of extraordinary faults.[4] Benteen's vindictive remarks can be partially explained by his reaction to criticism that he had failed to go to Custer's rescue in time at the Little Bighorn. Because Custer's view of the Little Bighorn River valley was obscured, he sent a detachment under Benteen to scout to his left. Benteen was later accused by some of having not made enough haste in seeking to rejoin Custer's forces. Furthermore, Benteen had a reputation for bitterness, jealousy and criticism of his fellow officers—even those with whom he was on good terms. Yet, his condemnation of Custer was by no means isolated. It was simply the most vitriolic evidence of the controversy that surrounded Custer and the events of his last campaign.

The most serious charges against Custer came after his death and connected his death and the death of 262 men under his command to Custer's alleged egotism and recklessness. For example, the senior surviving officer of the Seventh Cavalry, Maj. Marcus A. Reno, informed Sheridan that "Custer was whipped because he was rash."[5] The posthumous chorus against Custer included none other than President Grant. "I regard Custer's massacre as a sacrifice of troops," he told a reporter, "brought on by Custer himself that was wholly unnecessary—wholly unnecessary."[6] The press was all too eager to sensationalize on such remarks. "[A]s the tragic result has shown," one editorial charged, "not only all the substantial objects of the campaign, but the lives of nearly three hundred brave men were sacrificed to Custer's indiscretion, prompted by his eager thirst for personal notoriety."[7]

If Custer's critics were legion, so were his defenders. Within a year of Custer's death, his first biographer, Frederick Whittaker, soundly rejected the impression some had of Custer as a man of reckless abandon. Whittaker asserted that Custer calmly rose to the challenge of any emergency by making correct decisions under fire. Any mistakes made in the heat of battle were those of others. Whittaker also proclaimed that those weighing the facts would conclude that Custer was "the best cavalry leader America has ever produced."[8]

Whereas Custer's foes pointed to his last battle, his supporters often pointed back to his Civil war career. "He was not a reckless commander," one of his Civil War regimental commanders wrote. "He was cautious and wary, accustomed to reconnoiter carefully and measure the strength of an enemy as accurately as possible before attacking."[9] Even old foes shared these sentiments. Reacting to criticism in the press which attributed the Little Bighorn disaster to Custer, Thomas L. Rosser, a West Point classmate and Confederate general, remembered that "I never met a more enterprising, gallant or dangerous enemy during those four years of terrible war. . . ."[10]

If Benteen was the most violent critic of the commander of the Seventh Cavalry, Custer's greatest defender was his widow, Elizabeth Bacon Custer. Mrs. Custer devoted the rest of her life to defending her husband's reputation against those who she believed had failed or defamed him. Because of her status as a loyal and grieving widow, and by her enlistment of the support of noted army officers such as Nelson A. Miles, she effectively silenced many who attempted to uncover the truth behind the Custer mystery. So successful was Libbie Custer that by the time of her death in 1933, few survivors of the Little Bighorn were still alive and free to tell the real story.[11]

Whatever the conclusions about Custer, both the Washita and Little Bighorn campaigns were the result of certain post-Civil War army doctrines. The military had little respect for the Indians' fighting capabilities. Acting on the vague assumption that it could conduct "total warfare" (with the aid of technological superiority), the army failed to articulate a doctrine by which to conduct Indian warfare. Few coherent policies were developed other than preferences for winter campaigns, for the convergence of troop columns, and for cavalry over infantry. However, it was assumed that overwhelming resources, not superior strategy or skills, would supposedly decide the Indian question.[12]

The frontier army thus operated within a strategic void. Consequently, the army expected field commanders such as Custer to wage campaigns on an ad hoc basis. Generals such as Phil Sheridan not only allowed expedition commanders wide latitude but also assumed that separate military columns must be able to defeat any "hostile" Indians encountered. "No specific directions could be given," Sheridan concluded, "as no one knew exactly, and no one could have known where these Indians were, as they might be here to-day and somewhere else to-morrow."[13]

Ultimately, Sheridan, Custer, and virtually everyone else in the military recognized that the flight of their elusive targets was the one constant on which all decisions were based. After the Custer battle, Sheridan observed that "Indians seldom [make a] stand when the force is able to defeat them . . . [T]hey will scatter. . . ."[14] The failure of the [Winfield Scott] Hancock Expedition to accomplish anything against the Southern Cheyenne in 1867 and the fruitless pursuit of the tribe by the Seventh Cavalry that summer provided ample evidence of such frustrations and influenced the Washita Campaign the following year.[15]

The campaigns stemmed from the unsuccessful Medicine Lodge Creek Treaty of 1867, which had not brought peace to the Southern Plains. Raids by the Cheyenne (Tsistsistas) and other tribes against settlers and friendly tribes, such as the Pawnees, continued. The situation was aggravated by delayed ratification of the treaty.[16] Some Cheyenne chiefs, such as Black Kettle (Moketaveto) were in favor of peace, but they could not control the actions of some young men who went on the warpath north of the Arkansas River. Days before the attack on his village on the Washita, Black Kettle admitted to the military at Fort Cobb, Indian Territory, that "I have always done my best to keep my young men quiet, but some will not listen, and since the fighting began I have not been able to keep them all at home."[17]

The Southern Cheyenne had good reason to question the sincerity of the treaty and those sworn to uphold it. They could not easily forget the massacre of Black Kettle's village at Sand Creek in 1864 by the Third Colorado [State] Cavalry. In addition, they still felt betrayed by the seemingly pointless destruction of a village on the Pawnee Fork of the Arkansas River by the Hancock Expedition in 1867. This resentment and apprehension explained, in part, the continued unrest on the Southern Plains in 1868. However, such fears were of little concern to Major General Sheridan, who believed that security of the settlers and a permanent peace would not occur "unless the Indians are crushed out, and made to obey the authority of the government . . . ."[18] Sheridan had this goal in mind when he assumed command of the Military Department of the Missouri in 1868. The general's will, however, was easier expressed than accomplished. Years later, noted naturalist and folklorist George Bird Grinnell observed that the Army had forgotten one basic premise: the challenge was not so much to punish the Indians, but first and foremost to find and capture them.[19]

Throughout 1868 incidents involving warriors of the Cheyenne, Kiowa and other tribes went unchecked in western Kansas and eastern Colorado. Sheridan concluded that a winter campaign was necessary to neutralize the mobility of the hostiles. When fighting Indians in the summer, the Army, in his friend Custer's words, "had come off second best." If summer conditions allowed the Indians to remain elusive, the frontier Army's solution would be to use "so exacting and terrible an ally as the frosts of winter," a season when the Indian ponies were weakest. In addition, the need for more permanent encampments would force the Indians "to fight upon ground and under circumstances of our own selection."[20]

Sheridan described his concept of what might be termed "nineteenth century Cold War" in this way:

> The objects of the winter's operations were to strike the Indians a hard blow, and force them on to the reservations set apart for them, and if this could not be accomplished to show to the Indian that the winter season would not give him rest, and that he and his villages and stock could be destroyed; that he would have no security, winter or summer, except in obeying the laws of peace and humanity.[21]

Lieutenant Colonel Alfred Sully was in nominal command of the 1868-1869 winter campaign, but it was Sheridan who organized the expedition and assumed direct field control. Sheridan mobilized the U.S. Seventh Cavalry and the Nineteenth Kansas Cavalry for the campaign, with the Seventh selected as the strike force. Custer advised his wife of the new strategy: "The general [Sheridan] has finally decided upon a winter campaign. . . .[W]e are going to the heart of the Indian country, where white troops have never been before. The

Indians have grown up in the belief that soldiers cannot and dare not follow them there."[22]

Custer's goal was to catch the Indians unprepared in their winter camps, which were located south of the Arkansas River in Indian Territory (present-day Oklahoma). Unfortunately, the possibility existed that some of the bands that lived there in observance of the treaty might be affected as well.

In preparation for the rigors of such a campaign, Custer took steps to ensure that his regiment would be a disciplined, efficient organization when faced with battle. One step was organizing target practice twice a day.[23] Another was to form a units of sharpshooters. Referring to these actions, Custer noted, "The men are at target practice and it sounds like a battle."[24] Custer's training probably served his men well at the pending battle of the Washita. The Army, however, began to discourage target practice shortly after that, largely because it considered the expenditure of ammunition as wasteful. By the time the Seventh Cavalry fought at the Little Bighorn, enlisted men were expected to develop expertise in fire with only ten rounds of ammunition a month. The Little Bighorn battle graphically demonstrated the consequences of having under-trained men try to return fire for the first time. In fact, the Little Bighorn and Nez Perce Campaigns of 1876-77 convinced the Army to institute a comprehensive system of target practice and competitive matches.[25]

Custer's efforts to prepare the Seventh Cavalry before the Washita—which produced a more permanent army legacy than the arms training—included the distribution of a unique color of horse to each company . "All the horses of the regiment," Lt. Edward S. Godfrey wrote, "were . . . arranged according to color on one long picket line and each troop commander, according to rank, was given choice of color for his troop."[26] Gray mounts, for example, were assigned to "E" Company and the regimental band. (The "Gray Horse Troop," like some phantom, would remain a vivid memory of the battle of the Little Bighorn to the Sioux and Cheyenne for years after the battle.) Custer's decision also resulted in the redistribution of existing mounts, and not everyone was pleased with the result. Alfred Barnitz, for one, "bitterly opposed" the order to exchange his troop's horses to achieve the desired uniformity. "All my old horses," he complained to his diary, "were well trained . . . [T]he men were much attached to them, and now, just as we are to march on the campaign, everything is to be turned topsy turvey!" Barnitz predicted that the dissatisfaction created by Custer's "foolish, unwarranted, unjustifiable order" would lead to widespread desertion.[27]

Regardless of such misgivings, the reorganized Seventh Cavalry marched from its camp near Fort Dodge, Kansas, into Indian country on November 12, 1868. Realizing the difficulties of supplying troops in the field over long distances, Sheridan established a new base of operations one hundred miles south of Fort Dodge, near the junction of Wolf and Beaver Creeks.[28] On November 23, the regiment left "Camp Supply" in pursuit of its quarry. Custer later recalled that the band played "The Girl I Left Behind Me" in "a blinding snowstorm, with the wind in our faces, and through the soft snow a foot in depth."[29] The bad weather was "all the better for our purpose," Custer said to Custer Sheridan before his departure, "for we could move in it while the Indians could not."[30] A contingent of Osage and white scouts guided the 800 men of the regiment—eleven companies and the unit of sharpshooters—through enemy territory.[31]

Carrying rations for thirty days, Custer's regiment was to proceed south to the Canadian River.[32] His orders were necessarily general because the exact location of the enemy was unknown. His mission, though, was clear: find "the winter hiding-places of the hostile Indians and wherever found to administer such punishment for past depredations. . . ."[33] His goal approached realization on November 26 when a detachment under Maj. Joel Elliott made a discovery on the Canadian River. As Barnitz recalled it, "we came suddenly upon a plain, fresh trail, which obviously had been made in the afternoon of the day previous by a war party from one to two hundred Indians."[34] This trail headed southeast towards the Washita branch of the Canadian. Later, it would be determined that it was the trail of a Kiowa (K'uato) war party. It had arrived at Black Kettle's Cheyenne village the night before to warn the Cheyenne that army troops were in the vicinity. The Kiowa then returned to their own camp downstream. Their trail led Custer's column to Black Kettle's encampment, and the site thus became the object of Custer's attack.[35]

Custer's plan of attack for the dawn of November 27 was simple: the regiment would be divided into four detachments of equal strength in order "to completely surround the village and at daybreak . . . attack the Indians from all sides."[36] Although Custer intended that the band signal the attack, a shot fired from the village precipitated the assault. Despite this, many of Custer's units were in, or close to, their intended positions in time.[37] The Cheyenne were

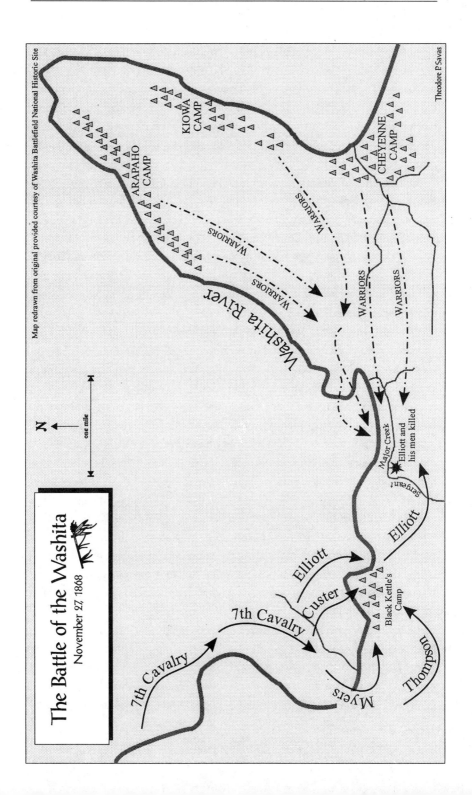

Map redrawn from original provided courtesy of Washita Battlefield National Historic Site

Theodore P. Savas

The Battle of the Washita
November 27 1868

N

one mile

Washita River

KIOWA CAMP

ARAPAHO CAMP

CHEYENNE CAMP

WARRIORS

WARRIORS

WARRIORS

WARRIORS

WARRIORS

WARRIORS

Major Creek

Elliott and his men killed

Sergeant

Elliott

Elliott

Custer

7th Cavalry

7th Cavalry

Myers

Black Kettle's Camp

Thompson

caught by surprise as the soldiers began to sweep through the camp with the regimental band playing "Gary Owen," a favorite amongst the men. According to Custer, "The Indians were caught napping for once." In addition to capturing the village of fifty-three lodges, with some fifty-three women and children, Custer later claimed that 103 warriors were killed in the encounter. Black Kettle and his wife were among the fallen. Survivors who eluded the troops fled to other camps downstream.[38]

Everything of value was destroyed, including arms and ammunition, the entire winter supply of buffalo meat, and most of the 875 captured horses and mules. Lieutenant Godfrey, whose troop had seized the herd, graphically remembered the horse slaughter years later: "We tried to rope them and cut their throats, but the ponies were frantic at the approach of a white man and fought viciously. My men were getting very tired so I called for reinforcements and details from other organizations were sent to complete the destruction of about eight hundred ponies."[39]

Cavalry casualties were light. Among the injured was Barnitz, who appeared to be mortally wounded by a Cheyenne bullet but survived.[40] Several men, including Major Elliott, were missing. Elliott was last seen pursuing a group of dismounted Indians down the valley, exclaiming: "Here goes for a brevet or a coffin!"[41] His remarks may have been dramatized in hindsight. If truly reported, they proved prophetic.

By good fortune, the Seventh Cavalry had struck only the westernmost of four widely separated Cheyenne, Arapaho, and Kiowa villages. However, Custer's attack at Black Kettle's village led to the abandonment of these other camps.[42] One of Custer's officers concluded that the Washita campaign "was a success from 'start to finish.'"[43] Though the survivors of Black Kettle's village would take exception to this observation, it was true from the Army's perspective. Sheridan's winter offensive would result in other hostile bands, including Satanta's Kiowas, reporting to the Indian agencies. It also included Custer's bloodless rescue of two white women held captive by the Cheyenne in the Texas panhandle.[44]

The campaign, however, bore ominous signs for the future. When Sheridan, Custer and the expedition returned to the Washita battlefield in December, they found the mutilated remains of Elliott and his detachment. "The bodies of Elliot and his little band," Custer reported, "with but a single exception, were all found lying within a circle, not exceeding 20 yards in diameter. We found them exactly as they fell, except their barbarous foes had stripped and mutilated the bodies in the most savage manner."[45] With the exception of Elliott, the men were buried in a hastily prepared grave on a small hill.[46]

Custer's alleged abandonment of Elliott exacerbated the strained relations between Benteen and Custer and fed an undercurrent of hostility in the Seventh Cavalry that lasted until the battle of the Little Bighorn. In a letter written to a friend in St. Louis, Benteen envisioned the men's deaths and condemned Custer's failure to search for Elliott's party before returning to Camp Supply. "There is no hope for that brave little band," he lamented, "the death doom is theirs, for the cavalry halt and rest their panting steeds. . . . No, they are forgotten."[47] After the letter appeared in the newspapers, Benteen claimed that Custer threatened before a group of officers to horsewhip the author. Admitting authorship, his revolver ready, the captain replied that he was ready to be whipped. "Custer," wrote Benteen, "wilted like a whipped cur."[48] Whether or not this incident occurred, one wonders what effect the fate of Elliott and the Washita letter might have had on Benteen's own alleged abandonment of Custer at the Little Bighorn.[49]

A well-documented episode with less apparent consequences occurred in March of 1869, when Custer rescued the previously mentioned female captives from the Cheyenne camp of Medicine Arrow on a tributary of the Red River. Entering the village with only Lt. William Cooke by his side, Custer attempted to obtain information concerning the two women. Escorted to Medicine Arrow's lodge, he participated in a peace pipe ceremony that involved the tribe's sacred "medicine arrows." The chief warned "Long Hair" (i.e., Custer) that he and his men would be killed if they harmed his people. He then poured ashes from the pipe on the toes of Custer's boots "to give him bad luck."[50] The curse was well-timed, as Custer later recalled that even while smoking he was planning how to capture the village.[51] To the Cheyenne, the prophecy of doom came true at the Little Bighorn. The Cheyenne observed that "it seemed he had not heard what our chiefs in the South said when he smoked the pipe with them."[52] The tribe would always believe that Custer's refusal to heed this warning was the cause of his death.[53]

The Washita Campaign of 1868-69 produced a formula that, in this author's opinion, should have ensured military success against Indian tribes of the Great Plains.[54] It called for a daybreak attack, the effective mobilization of troops, and a simultaneous attack by troop units of equal strength. Unsuspecting Indian encampments would have been hard pressed to defend against these tactics. This strategic formula, however, required a surprised and immobilized winter village, a circumstance which would not present at the Little Bighorn River in 1876.

The Great Sioux War of 1876-77 was partially due to the Federal government's inability or unwillingness to enforce the Fort Laramie Treaty of 1868 by preventing white gold seekers from invading the Black Hills area of the Great Sioux Reservation (modern western South Dakota). In addition, several bands of Lakota (a dialect group of "Sioux" speaking Indians) had never agreed to the terms of the treaty and to the ceding of their lands in Montana and Wyoming. Many of these Indians followed aggressive leaders such as Crazy Horse (Tashunca-Uitco) and Sitting Bull (Tatanka Iyotake). In an orchestrated attempt to precipitate military action against the "hostile bands," the Commissioner of Indian Affairs (with the Army's blessing) sent instructions in December of 1875 that all such groups had to report to their reservation agencies by January 31, 1876. The deadline came and went with little effect, and the War Department was ordered to force compliance.[55] It should be noted that winter weather, the Indians' general ignorance of the order, and the granting of but a few weeks' notice would have made it difficult for even willing Indians to comply with the December directive.

Sheridan, now a lieutenant general and in command of the Military Division of the Missouri, was once again in charge of operations. He issued instructions to brigadier generals George Crook and Alfred H. Terry, both Civil War veterans, to mobilize troops in their respective departments (the Platte and the Dakota). A preliminary thrust by Crook during the late winter in March 1876, enjoyed limited results.[56] The Northern Cheyenne he attacked fled to the village of Crazy Horse, and the two combined bands in turn joined forces with Sitting Bull's. Thus Crook's efforts helped spur the union of the various bands whose large camp Custer would later find on the Little Bighorn River in the Montana Territory[57]

A few months later Crook once again took the field from Fort Fetterman, Wyoming, and Terry organized his force at Fort Abraham Lincoln, Dakota Territory, and Fort Ellis, Montana. The column out of Montana was commanded by Col. John Gibbon, another Civil War combat veteran from the Army of the Potomac. The force out of Dakota was largely composed of troopers of the Seventh Cavalry, supported by units of the Sixth and Seventh infantry regiments. Custer had originally been assigned command of the Dakota column. However, he had incurred the displeasure of President Grant after testifying before a Congressional committee investigating charges of corruption in the Bureau of Indian Affairs.[58] Thus Alfred Terry assumed field command of the expedition, and Custer was relegated to leading the Seventh Cavalry. When the Dakota column left Fort Lincoln on May 17, 1876, bandsmen once again played "The Girl I Left Behind" and "Gary Owen."

The condition of the Seventh Cavalry in 1876, however, was not what it had been in 1867-1868. Eight years earlier the regiment was inexperienced, but boasted the advantages of recent physical and firearms training. In addition, its entire career to that time had been spent under a single leader, and it possessed a sense of unity and esprit that came from surviving a winter march. In 1876, the regiment had had little recent firing practice or field activity, had often seen its companies dispersed, and had been laboring under several short term commanders. Despite a popular perception that the Seventh was the foremost Indian fighting regiment in the frontier army, it had gained very little combat experience since the 1868-1869 Washita Campaign. Aside from minor engagements involving isolated detachments of the regiment, such as the Cheyenne attack on Fort Wallace in 1867, its military record was almost barren. Prior to the Battle at the Little Bighorn, the Seventh Cavalry had faced the Lakota Sioux only twice; both encounters were in 1873, and neither rose above the level of a light skirmish.[59]

Alfred Terry formulated his strategy after a scouting detachment discovered an Indian trail on Rosebud Creek that apparently led to the Little Bighorn.[60] The plan called for two columns to converge (one an attack force, the other a blocking force) against an Indian target believed to be on either the upper reaches of the Rosebud River or the Little Bighorn River.[61] The march of Gibbon's Montana column, southwards up the Bighorn River was intended to compliment the sweep of Custer's cavalry northwards via the valley of Rosebud Creek. Terry adopted the plan before he had effective operational intelligence as to his target. This can be regarded, once again, as demonstrating a preference for the type of troop convergence that had succeeded at the Washita. By the general's own admission, however, the exact location of "Sitting Bull's camp" was unknown when he sent Custer "in pursuit" of the Indians on June 22 with a force of 650 men.[62]

After the battle of the Little Bighorn, Terry charged that Custer disobeyed orders by attacking the Indian encampment before the anticipated arrival of Gibbon's column on the field. In a confidential dispatch to Sheridan on July 2, Terry alleged:

> The movements proposed by General Gibbon's column were carried out to the letter and had the attack been deferred until it was up I cannot doubt that we should have been successful. . . .The proposed route was not taken but as soon as the trail was struck it was followed . . . . I do not tell you this to cast any reflection on Custer for whatever errors he may have committed he has paid the penalty . . . but I feel that our plan must have been successful had it been carried out and I desire you to know the facts.[63]

Custer, in effect, was held responsible for the failure of Terry's plan and, therefore, for the failure of the expedition.

Although the cavalier's alleged egotism and reputation for recklessness seem to lend credence to Terry's charges, his accusations conflict with contemporary evidence. Several documents suggest that Terry himself left Custer the discretion to attack where and when circumstances warranted. Custer's last letter to his wife quoted that part of his orders which placed confidence in his judgment and allowed him to depart from these orders if he had "sufficient reason."[64] Also, Gibbon's chief of scouts, Lieutenant Bradley, noted in his diary on June 21 that "it is understood that if Custer arrives first, he is at liberty to attack at once if he deems prudent."[65]

Custer's orders reflected the lack of a coherent strategy that characterized the post-Civil War Army. Terry later acknowledged that the absence of "a known fixed objective point" had been a factor in the movements of Custer's and Gibbon's columns. Advising Sheridan of the anticipated movements of Custer and Gibbon, Terry admitted his uncertainty: "I hope that one of the columns will find the Indians."[66] The mobility of the enemy, the fear that they could and would escape, dominated the campaign and influenced the plan to send Custer "in pursuit." Pursuit, according to Gibbon, "was the idea pervading the minds of all of us. . . ."[67] Phrases in Custer's orders like "to preclude the escape of the Indians" reflected this obsession. Terry not only expected that Custer's numerically stronger force would "strike the Indians." He anticipated that Custer's cavalry "could pursue them if they attempted to escape."[68]

The preoccupation with pursuit may explain Custer's decision on June 25, 1876. The day before, his scouts confirmed that the trail led west to the Little Bighorn. Custer decided to follow the trail that evening and find the exact location of the village the next day (June 25). Once it was located, the regiment would surround and attack the village at daylight on June 26.[69] Custer's decision to push down the trail may have been influenced by the belief that the village was located closer to the mouth of the Little Bighorn than Terry's intelligence had indicated. If so, the village was an immediate threat to Gibbon's column.

Events on the morning of June 25 led Custer to discard his plan for an attack the next morning because he believed his presence had been discovered. Whether his conclusion was correct or incorrect does not matter, for the belief caused him to act prematurely. Custer was convinced that the element of surprise had been lost and that the Indians would escape. To prevent their flight, he concluded that he must attack at once, even though he was not convinced that his scouts had actually located the Lakota encampment in the valley of the Little Bighorn. According to Lieutenant Godfrey, Custer advised his officers that "our

View from high ground along Custer's route to the main village area in the Little Bighorn Valley. *C. Lee Noyes*

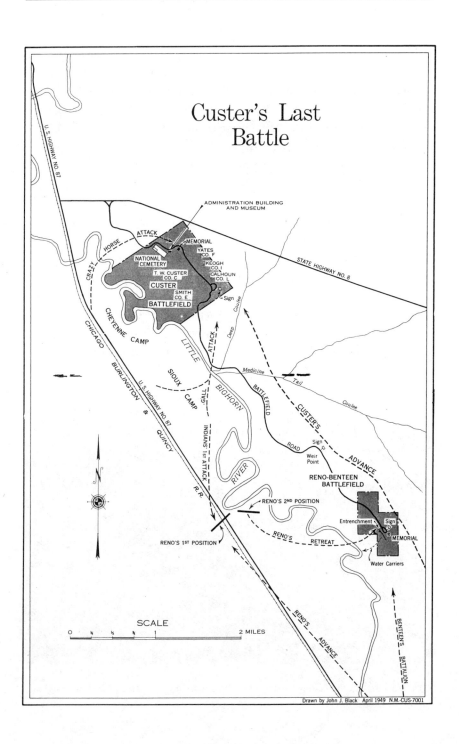

Custer's Last
Battle

ADMINISTRATION BUILDING
AND MUSEUM

U.S. HIGHWAY NO 87

STATE HIGHWAY NO. 8

ATTACK

HORSE

CRAZY

MEMORIAL

YATES
CO. F

NATIONAL
CEMETERY

KEOGH
CO. I

T. W. CUSTER
CO. C.

CALHOUN
CO. L

CUSTER

SMITH
CO. E.

BATTLEFIELD

Sign

CHEYENNE CAMP

CHICAGO

BURLINGTON &

LITTLE

SIOUX
CAMP

ATTACK

Deep Coulee

Medicine

Tail

BATTLEFIELD

BIGHORN

QUINCY

U.S. HIGHWAY NO. 87

INDIANS 1st ATTACK

R. R.

RIVER

ROAD

Coulee

CUSTER'S

Sign

Weir
Point

ADVANCE

RENO-BENTEEN
BATTLEFIELD

RENO'S 2ND POSITION

Entrenchment

Sign

MEMORIAL

RENO'S

RETREAT

Water Carriers

RENO'S 1ST POSITION

N

SCALE

0   ¼   ½   ¾   1   2 MILES

RENO'S   ADVANCE

BENTEEN'S   BATTALION

Drawn by John J. Black   April 1949   N.M.-CUS-7001

discovery made it imperative to act at once, as delay would allow the village to scatter and escape."[70] Another subordinate, Lt. Winfield S. Edgerly, further recalled that Custer's reason for dividing the regiment into four battalions was "to catch [the Indians] in whatever direction they might flee."[71]

The assumption that the Indians could and would flee influenced all subsequent decisions, including sending a battalion under Captain Benteen to scout to the left, and ordering another under Major Reno to attack down in the valley. As he observed the heavy clouds of dust in the valley, scout George Herendeen assumed that Custer "thought the Indians were moving away . . . for he sent Colonel Reno. . .[to] head for the dust. . . ."[72] The assumption of flight also influenced Custer's decision to suddenly move with his own division along the bluffs on the eastern side of the Little Bighorn.

Only when Custer reached the top of the bluffs did he locate what had been a vague, distant target or targets. Only then could he judge the size and strength of the encampment. To this day, students of the battle dispute the number of warriors present to defeat Custer. There is a growing tendency to be more conservative in the estimates. It is, in fact, possible that Custer was in the general vicinity of as many or more Indians at Washita than at the Little Bighorn. Yet, as Sheridan observed, "There certainly were enough Indians there to defeat the 7th Cavalry. . . ."[73] The strength, skill, and determination of the Lakota and Northern Cheyenne warriors at the Little Bighorn proved as important as their numbers.

The lack of a coherent strategy and the obsession with the Indian's mobility help explain the outcome of both the Washita and the Little Bighorn campaigns. At the Washita these factors help bring the Army success; at the Little Bighorn they brought failure. Custer was the same, but the character of his troops and the character of the campaign season in 1868 were very different from those in his 1876 expedition. At the Washita, Custer faced a sleeping winter encampment at dawn. The requirement that Plains bands disperse to seek firewood and the limited grazing available in winter had left the village too far from its neighbors for ready assistance. In addition, the snow, while hindering escape, had also limited pursuit. Moreover, Custer had by chance struck a band of Cheyenne that had been previously ravaged and discouraged by the massacre at Sand Creek, and its chief, Black Kettle, was eager only for peace. This had been Custer's only previous experience in attacking an Indian village.

At the Little Bighorn, Custer's detachment faced a fully aroused summer encampment in mid-afternoon. Also, the bands of Indians on the Little Bighorn was concentrated for unity, defense, and the conduct of religious ceremonies. While the Indians were better able to flee in summer than in winter, summer conditions also made it easier for the cavalry troopers to pursue anyone not on horseback. This meant that the women and children were especially vulnerable. The Indian warriors were obligated to attack if only to protect their families. Perhaps worst for Custer, their morale was at its height. They may have still been celebrating the defeat of Crook's column on the Rosebud River (June 21) when they routed Reno's detachment along the Little Bighorn. By the time they turned on Custer, many were confident of victory. At the Washita, resistance had been limited, and no counterattack had materialized. This time, however, the warriors not only stopped a concerted cavalry attack, but crushed it.

The most judicious evaluations of Custer reckon him not a rash man but a commander given vague orders, whose previous Indian encounters all suggested the worth of taking a calculated risk. Perhaps Custer was specifically

Little Bighorn Battlefield. The white markers on the knoll variously known as Custer Hill, Monument Hill, or "Custer's Last Stand" Hill mark the approximate locations where Custer and the men of Company F fell and were initially buried. The marker for Custer has a darkened inset. *C. Lee Noyes*

trying to apply the lessons he had learned at Washita at the Little Bighorn. If so, his victory at the Washita was also his downfall.

* The author wishes to express his appreciation to the following institutions, which provided valuable documentation for his article: Military Reference Branch, National Archives; Manuscript Division, Library of Congress; and the Little Bighorn Battlefield National Monument. A special acknowledgment is made to his partner, Michele.

NOTES

1. Sheridan to Mrs. Custer, April 10, 1865, in Marguerite Merrington, editor, *The Custer Story: The Life and Intimate Letters of General George A. Custer and His Wife Elizabeth* (Lincoln and London: University of Nebraska Press, 1987), 159. Mrs. Custer's literary executor and friend, Merrington heavily edited the letters she published and destroyed others.

2. The literature on Custer is voluminous. The most recent biographies include: Louise Barnett, *Touched by Fire: The Life, Death and Mystic Afterlife of George Armstrong Custer* (New York: Henry Holt, 1996); Robert M. Utley, *Cavalier in Buckskin: George Armstrong Custer and the Western Military Frontier* (Norman: University of Oklahoma Press, 1988); Jeffrey D. Wert, *The Controversial Life of George Armstrong Custer* (New York: Simon & Schuster, 1996).

3. Letters dated May 15, 1867, May 18, 1867, Robert M. Utley, editor, *Life in Custer's Cavalry: Diaries and Letters of Albert and Jennie Barnitz, 1867-1868* (New Haven and London: Yale University Press, 1977), 50-53. Noting Custer's harsh disciplinary action against six enlisted men who had left camp near Fort Hayes, Kansas, without a pass to purchase fruit, Barnitz recorded in his journal that Custer was "fast losing whatever little influence for good he may have once possessed in Regiment. . ." Ibid., 51, entry dated May 17, 1867. Benteen also referred to this and similar episodes at Fort Hayes. John M. Carroll, editor, *The Benteen-Goldin Letters on Custer and His Last Battle* (Mattituk and Bryan: J.M. Carroll & Company, 1974), 257-258.

4. Benteen to Theodore Goldin, November 17, 1891, February 17, 1896, Carroll, *The Benteen-Goldin Letters,* 205, 272. Elsewhere, Benteen asserted that "the regiment was in terrible shape from the very beginning, and Custer was the grand marplot [sic] and

cause of it all." Letter dated February 19, 1896, ibid., 273. In the author's opinion, rancor, rumor, and innuendo permeate these letters.

5. Reno to Sheridan, July 4, 1876, Sheridan, Library of Congress (hereafter LOC), Container 15 (MS 19,308). For an analysis of this and related issues, see C. Lee Noyes, "The Battle of the Little Bighorn: Reno, Terry and a Variation of a Major Theme," Northern Great Plains History Conference, Sioux Falls, South Dakota, October 1, 1998.

6. *New York Herald*, August 2, 1876. The *Herald* had, in turn, blamed Grant's "blundering" for the Little Bighorn disaster, ibid., July 7, 1876.

7. *St. Paul Pioneer Press*, July 8, 1876. This editorial accused Custer of sacrificing the public interest to "reckless ambition" and "personal vanity." See also ibid., May 11, 1876.

8. Frederick Whittaker, *A Popular Life of Gen. George A. Custer* . . . (New York: Sheldon Co., 1876), 610, 614. Whittaker blamed Reno and Benteen for the Little Bighorn massacre.

9. J. H. Kidd, *Personal Recollections of a Cavalryman With Custer's Brigade in the Civil War* (Grand Rapids: Black Letter Press, 1969), 132. Kidd had been colonel of the Sixth Michigan Cavalry. He admitted that these remarks were the "judgment of a friend and a loyal one."

10. *St. Paul Pioneer Press*, July 8, 1876. Rosser, in turn, criticized Reno for the Custer disaster. See also *New York Herald*, August 22, 1876.

11. In her efforts to defend her husband and keep his memory alive, Mrs. Custer published three books: *"Boots and Saddles"*; *or, Life in Dakota with General Custer* (1885); *Tenting on the Plains*; *or, General Custer in Kansas and Texas* (1887); and *Following the Guidon* (1890). On Mrs. Custer's role in the development of the Custer myth, see Shirley A. Leckie, "Gender as a Force in History and Biography: Examining the Custer Myth Through the Prism of Domestic Ideals," *North Dakota History,* LXIV (Fall 1997), 16-27; Nelson A. Miles, *Serving the Republic* . . . (New York and London: Harper & Brothers, 1911), 191-192. Lieutenant Edward S. Godfrey also defended Custer's actions at the Little Bighorn, arguing that his orders had given him "practically a free hand" in view of his Indian warfare experience. Edward S. Godfrey, "Custer's Last Battle," *Century,* XLIII (January 1892), 358-387. Godfrey commanded Company K at the Little Bighorn.

12. On the Army's failure to develop a consistent policy or effective strategy, see Robert Wooster, *The Military and United States Indian Policy, 1865-1903 (*New Haven and London: Yale University Press, 1988), and Perry Jamison, Crossing *the Deadly*

Ground: United States Army Tactics, 1865-1899 (Tuscaloosa and London: University of Alabama Press, 1994), 36-53.

13. Report dated November 25, 1876, in "Report of the Secretary of War [1876]," *House of Representatives Executive Document No. 1* (44th Cong., 2nd Sess.) Part 2, Volume I, 441 (hereafter *War, 1876.*)

14. Letter to Gen. William T. Sherman, August 10, 1876, Adjutant's General's Office (AGO), Letters Received (hereafter LR), National Archives and Records Division (NARA), RG 94, File 4163 AGO 1876 (4178 AGO 1876).

15. For an eyewitness account, see W. J. D. Kennedy, *On the Plains with Custer and Hancock: The Journal of Isaac Coates, Army Surgeon* (Boulder: Johnson Books, 1997). The best overview is Stan Hoig, *The Battle of the Washita: The Sheridan-Custer Indian Campaign of 1867-69* (Lincoln and London: University of Nebraska Press, 1976).

17. Captain Henry E. Alvord, "Record of a Conversation held between Colonel and Brevet Maj. Gen. W. B. Hazen . . . and chiefs of the Cheyenne and Arapaho tribes. . . ," November 20, 1868, in John M. Carroll, editor, *General Custer and the Battle of the Washita: The Federal View* (Bryan: Guidon Press, 1978), 32. Reprint of *Senate Executive Document No. 18* (40th Cong., 3rd Sess.). Black Kettle and Big Mouth, an Arapaho chief, had gone to Fort Cobb from their camps on the Washita to seek the protection of Colonel Hazen, who had been appointed agent for the southern tribes in the newly established reservation. Their efforts were unsuccessful, as Hazen advised them to return to their camps. "I cannot," he admitted, "stop the war." Ibid., 33. General Sherman, then commanding the Military Division of the Missouri, advised the Adjutant General on December 12, 1868, that "Black Kettle himself did not wish to be at war, but he had lost all control over his younger warriors. . . ." Ibid., 36. Sheridan was not so charitable in his annual report of November 11, 1869. AGO, LR, File 405 AGO 1870 (102 R 1870).

18. Sheridan, Annual Report, October 15, 1868, in Carroll, *Custer and the Washita*, p. 7.

19. Grinnell, *Fighting Cheyenne*, 288.

20. George A. Custer, *My Life on the Plains* (Lincoln and London: University of Nebraska Press, 1966), 262, 263. Benteen sarcastically referred to Custer's book as "Lie on the Plains." Letter dated February 22, 1896, Carroll, *Benteen-Goldin Letters*, 280.

21. Sheridan, Annual Report, November 11, 1868, File 405 AGO 1870 (102 R 1870).

22. Letter dated October 24, 1868, Elizabeth B. Custer, *Following the Guidon* (New York: Harper & Brothers, 1890), 13. Compare the condensed version dated "November 1868" in Merrington, *Custer Story*, 217.

23. Custer, *My Life on the Plains*, 265-269. As regimental adjutant in 1876, William Cooke died with Custer at the Little Bighorn.

24. Custer to his wife, October 24, 1868, cited above in note 22. See also John Gibbon, "Arms to Fight Indians," *United Service Magazine* (April 1879), 240. Gibbon lamented the enlistment of men "many of whom never looked through the sights of a rifle six months before they are called on to shoot Indians!"

25. See Douglas C. McChristian, *An Army of Marksmen: The Development of United States Marksmanship in the 19th Century* (Fort Collins: Old Army Press, 1981), 21-39. The records of the Ordnance Department contain extensive correspondence on this subject in the 1870s. Captain E. V. Sumner of the First Cavalry bemoaned the consequences of "men under fire for the first time" who "keep up a rapid and continuous fire, no matter in what direction, or to what effect." Letter to Chief of Ordnance, February 18, 1878, Office of the Chief of Ordnance, LR, NARA, RG 156, File 1074 OCO 1878.

26. Edward S. Godfrey, "The Washita Battle," Paul Andrew Hutton, editor, *The Custer Reader* (Lincoln and London: University of Nebraska Press, 1992), 161, reprinted from *Cavalry Journal*, XXXVI (October 1928). On November 3, 1868, Custer informed his wife that he had been "quite busy coloring the company horses. . . . [n]ow every company has one color." Custer, *Following the Guidon*, 14.

27. Utley, *With Custer's Cavalry*, 204, 205 (journal entries for November 10, November 11). Benteen also complained that the regiment had been "'colored' in the field at the beginning of the severest campaign that ever cavalry underwent." He implied that he had received the short end of the switch. Carroll, *Benteen-Goldin Letters*, 264.

28. Sheridan's report of November 1, 1869, File 405 AGO 1870 (102 R 1870); Custer, *My Life on the Plains*, pp. 273, 278-279.

29. Utley, *With Custer's Cavalry*, 213 (journal entry for November 23); also Godfrey, "The Washita Battle,"165.

30. Custer to his wife, November 22, 1868, Merrington, *Custer Story*, 219. The version of this letter which Mrs. Custer published does not contain this anecdote. *Following the Guidon*, 16-17. However, Custer's memoirs refer to this exchange, using almost identical language. *My Life on the Plains*, 283.

31. Little Beaver, leader of the thirteen Osage scouts, "[knew] the whole country South of the Arkansas." Sheridan to Custer, October 31, 1868, File 405 AGO 1870 (102

R 1870). White guides included Moses ("California Joe") Milner, Ben Clark and Jack Corbin.

32. Custer informed his wife on November 22 that his destination was "down the river to Fort Cobb, thence south-east towards the Washita Mountains, then north-west back to this point, my whole march not exceeding two hundred and fifty miles." Custer, *Following the Guidon*, 14-15.

33. Custer, *My Life on the Plains*, 280-281.

34. Utley, *With Custer's Cavalry*, p. 216 (journal reconstruction, January 7, 1869). Elliott's column consisted of Companies G, H, and M. Barnitz assumed that a war party had made the trail because "the Indians had no dogs with them, whereas hunting parties are always accompanied by dogs."

35. Philip McCusky to Col. Thomas Murphy, Superintendent Indian Affairs, December 3, 1868, Carroll, *Custer and the Washita*, 43. McCusky was the Kiowa and Comanche interpreter at Fort Cobb. However, Grinnell states that the war party was Cheyenne. "Some of the Cheyenne were going back to Black Kettle's village on the Washita, and some to other Cheyenne villages which were down below." *Fighting Cheyennes*, p. 290. In his annual report, Sheridan argued that Black Kettle's band had been guilty of recent raids on the Saline and Solomon Rivers.

36. Custer, *My Life on the Plains*, 321.

37. An account written for a newspaper circa 1889, in Utley, *With Custer's Cavalry*, 225.

38. Custer's report of November 28, 1868 ("In the Field, on Washita River"), File 405 AGO 1870 (102 R 1870). Even a liberal estimate of two warriors per lodge does not support Custer's claim that 103 warriors were killed. McCuskey reported that the Indians "acknowledge a loss of 11 Cheyenne (men) killed, including Black Kettle; the Arapahos had three men killed. . . ." Several women and children were also killed. See, however, citations 39 and 40 below.

39. Godfrey, "The Washita Battle," 174. Godfrey remembered that on the evening of November 28, "the officers were called together and each one questioned as to the casualties of enemy warriors. Every effort was made to avoid duplication. The total was found to be one hundred and three." Ibid., p. 175; see also Custer, *My Life on the Plains*, p. 380.

40. For Barnitz's account, see Utley, *With Custer's Cavalry*, pp. 226-227. A letter dictated to his wife on December 5 confirmed that 103 dead warriors had been found on the battlefield.

41. Godfrey, "The Washita Battle," 171.

42. Custer's report of November 28 noted that after his column had marched eight miles, it discovered that the other bands "had taken alarm at the fate of the Cheyenne village, and had fled." When the expedition returned to the scene in December, Sheridan further reported, there was evidence that the other villages "had fled in the greatest haste, abandoning provisions . . . and every species of property." File 405 AGO 1870 (102 R 1870). See also Custer, *My Life on the Plains*, 373.

43. Francis M. Gibson, "The Washita" (undated typescript), Gibson-Fougera Collection, Little Bighorn Battlefield National Monument (hereafter LBBNM), 56.

44. Custer, *My Life on the Plains*, 399-609; Frederick W. Benteen, "Hunting the Southern Cheyenne in the Spring of 1869 from Medicine Bluff Creek to El Llano Estacado" (undated mss, ca. 1891), Benteen Collection, University of Georgia Libraries, Athens (MS 770).

45. Custer's report December 22, 1868 ("In the field, Indian Territory"), File 405 AGO 1870 (102 R 1870).

46. David L. Spotts, a member of the Nineteenth Kansas Cavalry, recorded that Elliott was "buried separately on top of the mound with the men at his feet." *Campaigning With Custer, 1868-69* (Lincoln and London: University of Nebraska Press, 1988), 75. However, Custer reported that Elliott's body was not buried on the battlefield. Sixteen enlisted men, including Sgt. Major Walter Kennedy, died with Elliott.

47. Remarks made at Fort Cobb, I.T., Dec. 22, 1868, quoted in the *New York Times*, February 14, 1869 (originally published in the *St. Louis Democrat*). In an apparent defense of Custer's decision to withdraw from the field without a search, Sheridan argued that no one knew of Elliott's pursuit and no one heard the firing. "No one," he asserted, "knew of their exact fate until they were discovered some two weeks afterwards." Annual Report, November 1, 1869, File 405 AGO 1870 (102 R 1870). Gibson attributed the failure to notice Elliott's pursuit to "the excess of commotion and consequent excitement incident to a desperate hand to hand conflict. . . ." "The Washita," 43.

48. Benteen had written the letter to William J. DeGresse, "though I hadn't the remotest idea it would be published." Benteen to Goldin, February 17, 1896, Carroll, *Benteen-Goldin Letters*, 267.

49. Years later, Col. Richard Thompson remembered that before Custer's regiment marched to the Little Bighorn, "Benteen and Custer engaged in some personalities and recriminations. Benteen said that if they were to get into a fight he hoped he would be better supported than he was at the Battle of the Washita. . . . [I]t was plain to be seen that

Benteen hated Custer." Kenneth Hammer, editor, *Custer in '76: Walter Camp's Notes on the Custer Fight* (Provo: Brigham Young University Press, 1981), 247.

50. Grinnell, *The Fighting Cheyenne*, 296.

51. Custer, *My Life on the Plains*, 555-561.

52. Kate Bighead, as told to Thomas B. Marquis, "She watched Custer's Last Battle," Hutton, *The Custer Reader*, 376. Kate Bighead, a Southern Cheyenne, witnessed the Custer battle.

53. Interview with Long Forehead, better known as Willis Rowland, in Richard G. Hardoff, editor, *Cheyenne Memories of the Custer Fight* (Lincoln and London; University of Nebraska Press, 1998), 141-142.

54. In recognition of Custer's contribution to the success of the Washita Campaign, Sheridan promised to advance his protégé's career. "I will push your claims on the subject of promotion as soon as I get to Washington," he assured Custer on March 2, 1869, "and, if anything can be done, you may rely on me to look out for your interests (emphasis in the original)." Merrington, *Custer Story*, 228.

55. Documentation on the background of the Sioux War may be found in *Senate Executive Document No. 52* (44th Cong., 1st Sess.), and *House Executive Document No. 184* (44th Cong.). For an overall analysis of the Sioux War, see John S. Gray, *Centennial Campaign: The Sioux War of 1876* (Fort Collins: Old Army Press, 1876); Charles M. Robinson III, *A Good Year To Die: The Story of the Great Sioux War* (New York: Random House, 1995).

56. J.W. Vaughn, *The Reynolds Campaign on Powder River* (Norman: University of Oklahoma Press, 1961). Crook's longtime aide, Capt. John G. Bourke, provided an eyewitness account of the Powder River Battle. *On the Border With Crook* (London and Lincoln: University of Nebraska Press, 1971), 254-282. The military erroneously believed that the village was that of Crazy Horse.

57. Thomas B. Marquis, *A Warrior Who Fought Custer* (Minneapolis: Midwest Publishing Company, 1931).

58. On Custer's removal as expedition commander, see Sheridan's telegrams to Terry (April 28 and 29) and General William T. Sherman (April 29 and May 1). The Sheridan H. Papers (hereafter Sheridan), LOC (container 58), include copies of these telegrams logged in the general's dispatch book.

59. Utley, *Life in Custer's Cavalry*, 63-81, offers an account of the Fort Wallace skirmish, which involved Barnitz's Company G and a detachment of Company I.

60. Lieutenant James H. Bradley, *The March of the Montana Column: A Prelude to Custer Disaster* (Norman: University of Oklahoma Press, 1961), pp. 126, 142; Godfrey,

"Diary of the Little Big Horn," Vol. I (May 17-July 31, 1876), Edward S. Godfrey Papers (hereafter ESG), LOC (MS 7996); Edward S. Luce, editor, "The Diary and Letters of Dr. James M. DeWolf . . . ," *North Dakota History,* XXV (April-July 1958), 40, 81.

61. On the march of the Dakota Column, see Godfrey, "Custer's Last Battle," pp. 358-364. For the official itinerary, see the report of Terry's engineer officer, Lt. Edward Maguire, March 9, 1877, published in "Report of the Chief of Engineers to the Secretary of War for the Year 1877," *House of Representatives Executive Document No. 1,* Part 2 (45th Cong., 2nd Session), II, 1339-1349. (Hereafter *Engineers, 1877.*) On the location of the Indians, see Gibbon's dispatch to Terry of June 18, 1876, DD, LR, NARA, RG 393 File 3953 DD 1876; anonymous dispatch dated June 22, 1876, *New York Herald,* July 11, 1876. Captioned "A Voice From the Tomb," the *Herald* news item has been attributed to Custer.

62. Terry's Annual Report, November 21, 1876, *War 1876,* 461-462. Terry admitted that "it was impossible to make movements in perfect concert, as might have been done had there been a known fixed objective point to be reached. . . ."

63. Terry's report of July 2 may be found in various sources. The original telegram is located in Military Division of the Missouri, "Special File," NARA, RG 393, File 4241 MDM 1876. For the copy forwarded to the Adjutant General, see AGO, LR, File 3770 AGO 1876. The newspapers published this "confidential" dispatch before Terry's official report of June 27. The immediate effect of the July 2 dispatch was apparent when Sheridan advised the General of the Army: "Terry's column was sufficiently strong to have handled the Indians if Custer had waited for the junction." Telegram to Sherman, July 7, 1876, Sheridan, Container 58.

64. Letter to Mrs. Custer, 22 June 1876, 11 a.m., Elizabeth B. Custer, *"Boots and Saddles,"* 275-276. The Seventh Cavalry began its march up the Rosebud at noon that day.

65. Bradley, *March of the Montana Column,* pp. 143-144. Dispatch dated June 21, 1876 ("At Mouth of Rosebud"), *New York Herald,* July 11, 1876. Thomas L. Rosser expressed similar sentiments: "Gen. Custer was doubtless ordered to pursue them, cut off their retreat to the south, and to drive them back upon Terry and Gibbon, and thus hemmed in between these commands they were to be crushed." *St. Paul Pioneer-Press,* July 8, 1876.

66. Telegram to Sheridan, June 20, 1876, Military Division of the Missouri (hereafter MDM), "Special File," File 4035 MDM 1876.

67. Michael J. Koury, editor, *Gibbon on the Sioux Campaign of 1876* (Bellevue: Old Army Press, 1970), 22. "The Indians," Gibbon continued, "can always, in summer,

avoid a single column, or select their own time and place for meeting it. . . . The campaign of last year fully exemplified this." Ibid., 64.

68. Anonymous ("Custer's Battle Field, Little Horn, June 28"), *New York Herald*, July 8, 1876. This dispatch, attributed to Maj. James Brisbin, noted that Terry had decided that "Custer's column would strike the blow."

69. Lieutenant George D. Wallace, report dated January 27, 1877, *Engineers 1877*, 1377.

70. Godfrey, "Custer's Last Battle," 368.

71. "Some Facts In Regard to the Battle of the Little Big Horn" (undated typescript) in George Clark, editor, *Scalp Dance: The Edgerly Papers on the Battle of the Little Big Horn* (Oswego: Heritage Press, 1985), 16-17.

72. *New York Herald*, July 8, 1876. On the same note, Lieutenant Gibson informed his wife that Benteen's battalion had been "sent off to the left . . . to see if the Indians were trying to escape up the valley of the 'Little big horn.'" Letter dated July 4, 1876, Gibson-Fougera Collection, LBBNM; see also Walter Camp's undated interview with Godfrey, Hammer, *Custer in '76*, 75.

73. File 3770 AGO 1876 (6840 AGO 1877). The Army's alleged failure to appreciate the strength of the enemy became the standard explanation for what Sherman termed "the terrible calamity . . . by which General Custer and five companies of the 7th Cavalry perished." File 4163 AGO 1876 (4665 AGO 1877).

Did he save the balance of
the 7th Cavalry from annihilation,
or were his actions responsible
for the death of George
Armstrong Custer and 267 others?
It would be his destiny
to be forever –

In Custer's Shadow:
Major Marcus Reno

by
Ronald H. Nichols
Introduction by
Brian Pohanka

———

Volume 15 in the Source Custeriana Series

———

1000 copy printing
with more than 400 pages, over 60
photographs, and 11 maps, Ron Nichols has
given us the definitive look at Custer's
controversial second in command.
Available in a blue and white three piece
binding, 250 copy authors' autographed edition
ISBN 0-88342-069-4 . . . .$50.00

Regular edition in gold stamped, blue binding
ISBN 0-88342-068-6 . . . .$35.00

Available from:
The Old Army Press
P.O. Box 2243
Fort Collins, CO 80522
or order toll free 1-800-627-0079

Archaeological Evidence

The Attack on Black Kettle's Village on the Washita River

William B. Lees

In reporting his victory over Napoleon at Waterloo, the Duke of Wellington observed that "[n]othing except a battle lost can be half so melancholy as a battle won."Perhaps the same can be said of the campaigns of archaeologists. Dr. Bill Lees has been involved in the search for the two different locations at which Black Kettle's Cheyennes were cut down. One site, that of the Sand Creek Massacre (1864), apparently remains lost. The other field, the attack at the Washita River, was successfully found. However, as Dr. Lees notes in his conclusion, the archaeologists experienced some disappointments even in their "victory" at Washita.

In 1995 and 1997, the Oklahoma Historical Society conducted archaeological surveys of land in Roger Mills County believed to be the site of the November 27, 1868, attack on Black Kettle's village by the United States Seventh Cavalry Regiment. The goal of the archaeological project was to determine whether this assumption was correct and, if so, to establish the location of the village and other places associated with the attack. Funding and assistance with this project were provided by the National Park Service through their American Battlefield Protection Program, Midwest Archeological Center, and Southwest Region office.

The areas surveyed during these projects included most of the land now owned by the National Park Service (the new Washita Battlefield National Historic Site), private lands located immediately west of the park land, and parcels of land along Sergeant Major Creek on the northwest edge of the town of Cheyenne. The land along Sergeant Major Creek was searched for evidence that might indicate the site of the demise of Maj. Joel H. Elliott's detachment of troops from the attacking forces.

Methods

The archaeological methods used at the Washita battlefield were developed by the National Park Service during their mid-1980s research at the Little Bighorn Battlefield National Monument, Montana. These same methods have since been used effectively at other battlefields of the Indian wars, American Revolutionary War, Mexican War, and American Civil War.

The approach used at the Washita site involved several steps:

1) Working as a team, volunteers equipped with metal detectors systematically scanned the study area for artifacts. When their metal detectors indicated the presence of a metal object buried in the ground or on the surface, that place was marked with a surveyor's pin flag;

2) A recording crew followed behind the metal detectors, excavated the artifacts, and collected those that related, or possibly related, to the 1868 event. In the process, they assigned each collected artifact a unique identification number;

3) Using electronic surveying equipment, a survey crew recorded the precise location of each collected and numbered artifact.

Through this process, a precise map was made showing the location of each attack-related artifact (see map on next page). By using this map and by accurately identifying the artifacts found, it is possible to detect patterns in the location of the artifacts that may reveal information about the event.

The Artifacts

Each of the artifacts discovered helps us to understand the Washita site because it gives us a clue to where a person, if only for a moment, was located. A fired cartridge case ejected from a Spencer carbine (a short, light cavalry

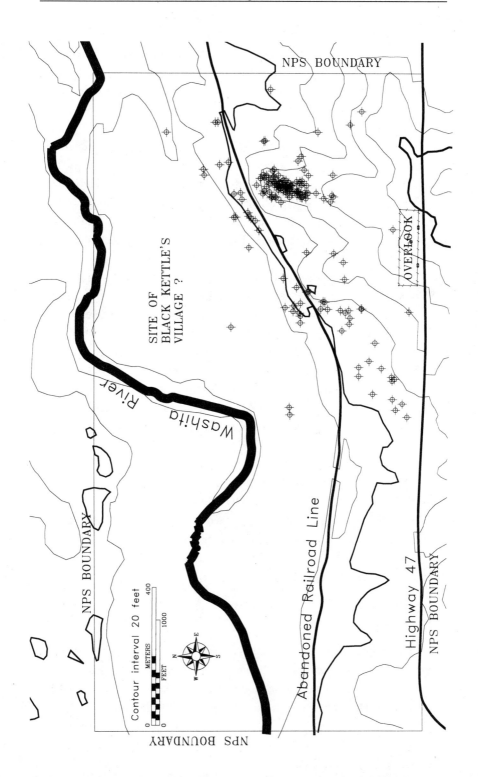

SITE OF
BLACK KETTLE'S
VILLAGE ?

NPS BOUNDARY

NPS BOUNDARY

NPS BOUNDARY

NPS BOUNDARY

OVERLOOK

Washita River

Abandoned Railroad Line

Highway 47

Contour interval 20 feet

METERS
FEET

weapon) falls to the ground near the soldier who pulled the trigger. When, over a century later, that same cartridge is found, it still marks that soldier's approximate location. The bullet fired from the carbine also marks, though less directly, the location of a human target as it too finds its way to the ground somewhere near that target.

During the two weeks of the survey, the participants collected a total of 190 artifacts that were felt to be certainly or possibly related to the attack (see Artifact Table on page 34). Most of these artifacts were ammunition for a variety of weapons. The majority of them belonged to the U.S. Seventh Cavalry. In all, 155 of the 190 artifacts found in 1995 and 1997 are fired and unfired metal cartridges for Spencer carbines. The Seventh Cavalry was equipped with the Spencer and also with either Remington or Colt revolvers that used .44 caliber ammunition. In addition, cartridge cases used for the Henry carbine and the Springfield Model 1866 rifle (.50-70 caliber) were found on the site, and these also appear to date to the 1868 attack. (Ammunition of .44 caliber was .44 inches or 1.1 centimeters in diameter; ammunition that was .50-70 was .50 inches or 1.3 centimeters in diameter and used a 70 gram powder charge.)

These cartridges provide us with an unusual ability not only to tell where combatants were located on the site, but to identify where different *individuals* were located. This is possible because the firing pins of different types of weapons leave identifiable marks on the cartridge. Not only is the firing pin mark of a Henry distinct from that of a Spencer, for example, but the firing pin of each weapon has a unique signature that can be used to distinguish one gun from all others of the same type. Firearms identification analysis of the cartridges conducted by Douglas D. Scott of the National Park Service allowed him to identify cartridges fired in thirty-seven different Spencers. He was also able to conclude that all seven Henry cartridges found were fired from the same weapon, and that the four Springfield Model 1866 (.50-70) cartridges were likewise fired from a single rifle.

Patterns

An examination of the placement of artifacts on the site reveals a number of interesting patterns. The first is the general location of artifacts discovered during the surveys. Except for a single fired Spencer cartridge case, all the artifacts related to the event were found within the park boundary, most within the southeastern portion of the National Historic Site (NHS). The single cartridge discovered outside of the NHS was found along Sergeant Major Creek and may relate to the movement of Joel Elliott's detachment. While it is important to remember that no survey was conducted on lands adjacent to the NHS on the north, east, or south, it is significant that no relevant artifacts were found in the western half of the NHS or adjacent to and west of the NHS along the Washita valley. This seems to contradict claims that Black Kettle's Village was located slightly west of the NHS.

It is also important to note that virtually no evidence of fighting or of a village (in the form of metal "camp debris") was found on the floodplain of the Washita River. However, based on preliminary geomorphological research conducted by C. Vance Haynes of the University of Arizona, the absence of artifacts on the floodplain appears to be the result of the destruction of the 1868 surface by natural processes of erosion. If this is true, no direct evidence for the location of Black Kettle's village may exist.

The evidence of fighting that does exist on NPS land provides useful insight into the attack of November 27, 1868. Most of the artifacts appear to be associated with a group of some thirty-six troopers of the Seventh Cavalry. Spencer cartridges fired by these cavalrymen are found over the entire southeastern quadrant of the NHS. All but five of the troopers were also at one time or another positioned on a prominent ridge overlooking the floodplain of the Washita River (a location marked by the densest concentration of artifacts on the map reproduced on page 31). The evidence indicates that these troopers either congregated on this ridge from a wider area, or were positioned on this ridge and ranged out from it in all directions.

Analysis of the dispersion of cartridges on the ridge does not reveal a grouping that would have resulted from troopers being positioned in formal skirmish lines. Maintaining a formal skirmish line would have resulted in somewhat tight clusters of cartridges along a line. Rather, the pattern on the ridge, as well as evidence that the troopers traveled in all directions either to or from the ridge, shows a much more informal organization characterized by fluid movement. This pattern may suggest how different tactical discipline was within the years immediately following the Civil War when contrasted with the evidence of the Seventh Cavalry's late use of formally executed skirmish lines at the Little Bighorn.

Artifacts thought to relate to the attack on
Black Kettle's Village, November 27, 1868,
and discovered during archaeological surveys in 1995 and 1997

Description of artifacts	Probable association	Number found in 1995 survey[1]	Number found in 1997 survey[2]
Spencer cartridge cases	U.S. 7th Cavalry	107	10
Spencer cartridges (unfired)	U.S. 7th Cavalry	14	13
Spencer bullets (fired)	U.S. 7th Cavalry	11	-
Henry cartridge cases	U.S. Scout/Officer	7	-
.50-70 cartridge cases	U.S. Scout/Officer	4	-
ca. .50 caliber spherical bullets	Native American	6	-
.36 caliber conical pistol bullets	Native American	1	1
.44 caliber spherical pistol bullets	U.S. or Native American	3	1
.44 caliber conical pistol bullets	U.S. or Native American	1	2
Lead shot bar	Native American	1	-
Iron harness hardware	U.S. or Native American	3	2
Military buttons	U.S. or Native American	2	-
Civilian button	Native American	1	-
Totals		**161**	**29**

1   Donated by landowner Betty Wesner to the National Park Service, November 1, 1997.

2   Property of the Oklahoma Historical Society.

It is also important to note that the seven cartridges from the single Henry carbine were all found within the dense cluster of Spencer cartridges on the ridge. Of the four Springfield Model 1866 (.50-70) cartridges, two were also found within the ridge cluster, and the other two also within areas where Spencer cases were found. The proximity of the Springfields to the Spencers suggests very strongly that the Springfields were carried by either officers or scouts with the Seventh Cavalry.

Little physical evidence was found for the Indian response to the U.S. attack. The few artifacts unearthed consisted of a .36 caliber revolver bullet, seven .50 caliber lead balls, a lead shot bar, and possibly some buttons and tack; unfortunately, they do not reveal clear patterns that will help in interpreting the event. The seven .44 caliber bullets fired from revolvers may have come from Indian weapons, but they more likely originated with the Seventh Cavalry.

Conclusions

Archaeological survey of most of the land contained within the new Washita Battlefield National Historic Site, as well as additional lands, has revealed only limited evidence of the 1868 attack on Black Kettle's Village. Most of the evidence apparently resulted from the operation of one company of the Seventh Cavalry, with meager evidence of the Indian response to the attack. This company of soldiers appears to have been positioned on a ridge overlooking the Washita River floodplain. Two officers and/or scouts, armed with a Henry and a Springfield Model 1866, were apparently among these troopers. A number of .44 caliber bullets fired from Colt Model 1861 revolvers may be associated with these troopers or, somewhat less likely, with the besieged Indians.

The organization of the troopers seems to have been informal. There is no evidence for the use of formal skirmish lines, and the troopers appear to have either congregated on the ridge from different directions or to have almost randomly moved around this ridge and out from it in all directions. It is possible to explain the presence of troopers on this ridge as either offensive or defensive. Early in the day's fighting, troopers positioned on this ridge could easily have been facing the floodplain and Black Kettle's Village. Later in the day, they could have been facing to the southwest to resist increasing pressure from

Indians who were harassing the Seventh Cavalry, eventually forcing its withdrawal.

The research to date leaves many unanswered questions about this action. The location of Black Kettle's village, for example, remains undiscovered, as does the location of the majority of the Seventh Cavalry and the majority of the Indian combatants. Some of this evidence is probably missing because of the erosive action of the Washita River since 1868. Other evidence certainly remains to be found on lands beyond the NHS boundary to the north, east, and south. Until other physical evidence of the encounter is documented using scientific methods, we can only speculate on the circumstances surrounding the thirty-six troop positions recently discovered in Roger Mills County.

Select Bibliography

Fox, Richard Allan, Jr. *Archaeology, History, and Custer's Last Battle: The Little Bighorn Revisited.* Norman: University of Oklahoma, 1993.

Haecker, Charles M. *A Thunder of Cannon; Archaeology of the Mexican-American War Battlefield of Palo Alto.* Southwest Cultural Resources Center Professional Papers No. 52. National Park Service, 1994.

Haecker, Charles M. and Jeffrey G. Mauck. *On the Prairie of Palo Alto: Historical Archaeology of the U.S.-Mexican War Battlefield.* College Station: Texas A & M University, 1997.

Haynes, C. Vance, "Late Quaternary Geology of the Washita Battlefield: A Tentative Assessment." Manuscript on file, Historic Sites Division, Oklahoma Historical Society, Oklahoma City, 1995.

Lees, William B. "Archaeology of the Mine Creek Civil War Battlefield, Linn County, Kansas." Report prepared for the Kansas State Historical Society, on file at the Kansas State Historical Society, Topeka, 1998.

———. "When the Shooting Stopped, the War Began," in *Look to the Earth: Historical Archaeology and the American Civil War*, ed. by Clarence R. Geier, Jr., and Susan E. Winter (Knoxville: The University of Tennessee Press, 1994), 39-59.

———. "An Historic Burial from the Southern Plains," *Plains Anthropologist* 37 (1992), 213-231.

McChristian, Douglas C. to Bob Rea, Fort Supply Historic Site, July 19, 1996, on file at Fort Supply Historic Site, Oklahoma Historical Society, Fort Supply, Oklahoma.

Scott, Douglas D., "Firearms Identification Analysis of Cartridge Cases from the Washita Battlefield." Manuscript on file at the Oklahoma Historical Society, Historic Sites Division, Oklahoma City, 1997.

——, Richard A. Fox, Jr., Melissa A. Connor, and Dick Harmon. *Archaeological Perspectives on the Battle of the Little Bighorn.* Norman: The University of Oklahoma, Norman, 1989.

Jerry L. Russell, Founder and National Chairman

THE STUDY OF THE MILITARY HISTORY of the early settlement of North America, and the continuing conflicts between Indian and Indian, Indian and settler, Indian and soldier, has long been a subject that has fascinated succeeding generations of Americans.

In the early decades of this century, an organization known as **The Order of Indian Wars of the United States**, made up primarily of retired military men, actual veterans of the Indian Wars, devoted its attention to the study of the U.S. military establishment's role in the development and settlement of this country's westward-moving frontier. That organization became an affiliate of the American Military Institute in 1947, and is once again active for descendants.

IN 1979, WE FOUNDED A **NEW** ORGANIZATION, inspired by that other group--a "spiritual descendant," if you will--but having no connection, official or otherwise with the predecessor. Our purpose, however, is similar--but broader: the in-depth study and dissemination of information on America's frontier conflicts. We are as interested in the "Indian side" as in the "Army/settlers side," although this organization, and its Assemblies, are not to be a forum for political or sociological crusades or guilt trips---our interest is in **military history**.

An additional purpose, equally important, we believe, is our concern for the historic preservation of those important sites associated with the history of the Indian Wars in America. Citizens' groups **must** become more involved in historic preservation, or much of our past will be irretrievably lost, in the name of 'progress'. Historic military sites are an important part of our national heritage, and the preservation/protection of these sites will be a major, continuing, concern of our organization--hence our motto: WE WHO STUDY MUST ALSO STRIVE TO SAVE! HERITAGEPAC is the national lobbying organization established in 1989 to work for preservation of battlesites. Our main publication is the *OIW Communique*.

DUES ARE $20 A YEAR.

Our 21st Annual National Assembly, Focusing on the 125th Anniversary of The Red River War, will be held September 16-18, 1999, in Amarillo, Texas, With Tours Led By Neil C. Mangum, Superintendent, Little Bighorn Battlefield, to Adobe Walls, Palo Duro Canyon & The Washita Battlefield, Plus 12 Speakers.

WRITE FOR INFORMATION.
Order of the Indian Wars
P. O. Box 7401, Little Rock AR 72217
501-225-3996   > indianwars@aristotle.net <

Washita Battlefield

An Introduction to a National Historic Site

Sarah L. Craighead

Washita Battlefield National Historic Site in Oklahoma, one of the newest units of the U.S. National Park Service, protects and interprets the site of the Southern Cheyenne [Tsistsistas] village of Black Kettle that was attacked by the U.S. Seventh Cavalry under the command of Lt. Col. George A. Custer just before dawn on November 27, 1868. Troopers attacked the fifty-seven Indian lodges, killing a number of men, women, and children. Custer reported about 100 Indian dead, although Indian accounts claimed that only eleven warriors and nineteen women and children lost their lives. Fifty-three Cheyenne women and children were captured and detained until the following summer. Custer's own losses included two officers and nineteen enlisted men killed.

The cavalry strike was hailed at the time by the military and by many civilians as a significant victory aimed at reducing Indian raids on white frontier settlements. The event at Washita River remains controversial because many Indians and whites, both then and now, have labeled Custer's attack a "massacre." The policy decision of the U.S. Army to launch surprise attacks on entire villages whenever they were vulnerable polarized the Indians of the southern Plains. Some gave up any hope of resistance to white settlement. Others, vowing never to submit, met Custer one last time, at his fatal battle at the Little Bighorn River in Montana in 1876.

The larger story of the Washita Campaign epitomizes the ethical dilemma of trying to resolve cultural conflict through military means. It is a story of non-Indian western expansion, of whites' perceived "manifest destiny," and of

Superintendent Sarah Craighead at Washita Battlefield National Historic Site. *Michael A. Hughes*

using winter campaigns as a military tactic to force the Indians onto reservations. To the Cheyenne people, the battlefield park is a deeply meaningful place with spiritual significance; it is a place to show respect for lives lost and provides a wonderful opportunity for both healing and education.

Washita Battlefield was established as a national historic site on November 12, 1996. The area was recognized as a location of national significance by being designated a national historic landmark as early as 1965. The state of Oklahoma administered a three-acre overlook area at the site until national historic site status became a reality. [Editor's note: Sites designated as national historic landmarks in the U.S. are similar to what are termed national historic sites in Canada—places recognized by the federal governments as having national significance but which are frequently not part of the federal park system.] The remainder of the 300-acre battlefield was privately owned until the summer of 1997, when private donors and the state of Oklahoma purchased the property and donated it to the National Park Service. The Cheyenne and Arapaho tribes and the Oklahoma Historical Society are included in park legislation as partners in park development. The National Park

Service will continued to work with these as well as other critical partners in the years to come.

Short and long term planning are occurring simultaneously at this new unit of the park service. A successful symposium on the park's past, present, and future was held in Cheyenne November 13-14, 1998. Park rangers began leading walks and programs on site this summer. A temporary interpretive trail is in place, and a brochure is being developed so that visitors can experience the park on their own. Park staff are working with the Oklahoma Historical Society to upgrade exhibits in the society's Black Kettle Museum in the town of Cheyenne, so that it can serve as a visitor contact point until construction of a National Park Service museum and visitor center. The upgrade will provide the public with a quality visit by displaying modern exhibits that reflect present day-attitudes and information about the Battle of the Washita, the Indians that lived there, and the reasons why this event was so pivotal in American history.

Long range plans include creation of a General Management Plan (GMP), which will guide overall development of the park. The park's GMP will help to

A recent tour group descending Custer Knoll at Washita Battlefield National Historic Site. *Michael A. Hughes*

determine the location and size of buildings, trails, and other park facilities. The GMP should be completed within the next two years.

The National Park Service now has the incredible challenge of not only preserving a hallowed place but also presenting it to the public in a way that is balanced, sensitive, and provocative. Washita Battlefield National Historic Site has the potential to provide all people with an opportunity to learn about our heritage through a single event in American history that has touched us all, both then and now.

Kicking Bear's Canvas

A Warrior-Artist's Account of the Battle of the Little Bighorn

Rodney G. Thomas

For six generations, the valley of the Little Bighorn River has kept its secrets well. On a June morning in 1876, haze, foliage, and slopes obscured the view of the last Indian village that George A. Custer would ever see. For the next century, the wiry sod walked upon by thousands of visitors concealed a wealth of physical evidence of the battle, only to be unexpectedly revealed through a grass fire in 1983. Similarly, assumptions about the artistic and conceptual limitations of Plains Indians still prevent much about the battle in the valley from being revealed. An example is the continued lack of appreciation for the historical value of a painting produced by the warrior-artist Kicking Bear.

Kicking Bear's portrayal of the battle of the Little Bighorn is today one of the most reproduced pieces of American Indian art. It adorns book covers, magazine articles, and brochures. Yet it has not been appreciated for what it is—a genuine documentary of the battle, but one told through Indian eyes.

Kicking Bear (Mato Wanartaka) was born around 1846 and was Oglala Lakota—Lakota is a major division and dialect group of the "Sioux" speaking peoples—by birth. He later married into a Minneconjou family and was a band leader in that branch of the Lakota nation. As such, he fought against both Reno's and Custer's battalions at the Little Bighorn (the Indians' "Battle of the Greasy Grass"). He is prominently portrayed in Amos Bad Bull's ledgerbook art rendition on the battle and is depicted with that artist's father at the start of the fight against Reno's advancing battalion.[1] Kicking Bear became even more famous later, in the waning years of his nation's strength. He and Short Bull were the two Lakota warriors who made the trek to Nevada to assess a Paiute

(Numu) visionary named Wovoka and his message. Kicking Bear would play a significant part in spreading Wovoka's messianic and apocalyptic religion, which would go down in history as the "Ghost Dance Movement." After the 1890 Wounded Knee massacre halted the movement, Kicking Bear was arrested and held in jail in Fort Sheridan, Illinois, for a year. In 1891, he was set free to join Buffalo Bill's Wild West Show on a tour to Europe. Disgusted with this humiliating experience, Kicking Bear went back to the Pine Ridge Reservation of modern South Dakota to live out his life with his family.

Between 1893 and his death in 1904, a rather steady stream of visitors came by Kicking Bear's cabin to talk of the old days. He was also frequently photographed, and on one visit to Washington, D. C., Smithsonian anthropologists made a life mask of him. This was used by a local sculptor as the mold for fifty-six heads of Kicking Bear placed on the Q Street Bridge in Rock Creek Park in Washington.[2] The old warrior passed away on May 28, 1904, near Manderson, South Dakota, unrepentant for holding to tradition and a hero still to his people. His death was one more sign of the dying of the old ways.

Kicking Bear's version of the Battle of the Little Bighorn was made at the request of Frederic Remington and was completed in 1898. For some reason, Remington did not take possession of the painting despite having paid for it. Irvin S. Cobb, one of the most popular fictional writers in America during the 1930s and 1940s, eventually acquired it. After Cobb's death, the painting was donated to its present owner, the Southwest Museum in Los Angeles, California. To the best of this author's knowledge, no one has yet analyzed this painting on any other basis than its style and aesthetic or provided any more than a simple description of its contents.[3]

Displayed as *Battle of the Little Big Horn*, the work is painted on a muslin sheet with watercolor and is 3 feet (.9 meters) wide and 5 feet (1.5 meters) long. There is a surprising lack of information on this painting in spite of its popularity and frequent reproduction. A label attached to the frame by Cobb provides the only known information on the painting's origin.[4] The label also contains some interpretative notes that present the sum knowledge of all that is allegedly depicted in the painting. The text on the label is given below:

> Kicking Bear's pictograph done at Pine Ridge Agency, about 1898. Twenty odd years after the event, this old sub-chief of the Sioux finally consented to do his version of the Battle of the Little Big Horn in 1876. Up until that time his native caution and conservatism—perhaps also a mistaken

fear of retaliation or punishment by the Whites—had stayed his hand. One of his few friends among the whites, Frederick [sic] Remington, the artist, finally induced him to make this painting. Kicking Bear worked on the task all one winter. When Remington failed to appear in the following spring—and forgot to write even—the old chief became aggrieved. He sold the work to the resident [Indian] agent, whom he liked. It was the agent who, at Kicking Bear's request, wrote in the names of the depicted leaders on the Indian side and the names of the Sioux warriors who fell in the battle.

In 1902 the agent sold the picture to George Rehse, also an artist, from whom I purchased it in 1934. Interesting details: Chief Gall is omitted from the central group showing Rain-In-The-Face, Crazy Horse, Sitting Bull, and of course, in a prominent place, Kicking Bear. This was done deliberately because Gall had affiliated himself with the reconciled Sioux whereas Kicking Bear, like Sitting Bull, remained hostile and unreconstructed all his life. So Kicking Bear leaves blank the space where Gall, as head chief, should be shown. The artist shrewdly forbears to show the mutilation of the fallen whites, but presents himself as having just lifted the scalp of one of Custer's Indian Scouts. The slain Custer is shown wearing his hair long and in his favorite buckskin costume. The Indians called him "Long Hair." The uncolored outlines, shown in one corner, are supposed to represent the spirits escaping from the bodies of those who have just died or still are dying. This corner purports to be the spot where the last Indians fell and bursts of gunfire still come from the margin to show that the Indians are continuing their volleys.

In the lower diagonal corner is the Indian village where the women are beginning the Victory Chant and even the dogs join in the jubilation. One woman displays a captured American flag. Kicking Bear was one of the two emissaries sent by the Sioux to test the validity of the claim of the "Paiute Messiah," who first preached the doctrine of the Ghost Dance in the last great uprising of the Plains Tribes. He endorsed the new faith and his people embraced it—with the result that Big Foot's band was exterminated by our cavalry at the Massacre of Wounded Knee and Sitting Bull was killed while resisting arrest at the hands of Indian policemen sent from the reservation to make a prisoner of him. The Government authorities regarded Kicking Bear as a chronic trouble-maker. His own people called him a patriot and gallant warrior. Soldiers who fought against him gave him credit for courage and shrewdness.

Irvin S. Cobb.[5]

It is unlikely that the the information on the painting's label originated with Cobb, the painting's owner. The note was produced by someone with some detailed knowledge of the battle and of the Indians participants. Cobb, however, was hardly an ethnologist, and it is unlikely that he had access to interpretive assistance from members of Kicking Bear's tribe on the Pine Ridge Reservation. Cobb's understanding of what the painting represented could have come from three possible sources. The first was the Pine Ridge Indian agent who might have not only noted the Indian names on the painting, but also recorded Kicking Bear's narrative concerning the painting's contents and background. The second was George Rehse, who could conceivably have passed along to Cobb his interpretation of what he had been told of the painting. The third possibility was E. A. Brininstool, one of the original Little Bighorn aficionados and a well-known journalist and author. Brininstool was a resident of Los Angeles at the same time as Cobb; the two men might have met and discussed the painting. While speculative, such a meeting is certainly possible given the fame of both men and their common interests.[6]

Kicking's Bear's painting is an example of artwork done in the distinctive Indian pictographic style. In this style, the artist used simple, stylized drawing or incising to portray a subject. Pictographic style art had a variety of purposes. It was generally decorative—the Plains Indians, in particular, had long used this art style to decorate shields, tepees, clothing, robes, etc. But pictographic art was also used to record and proclaim important events and to assist the artist in retelling the stories of those events. Lewis and Clark were among the first to see and mention pictographic art, and the painter George Catlin recorded several examples in his Indian portraiture a few decades after that.[7]

It was not until the latter half of the nineteenth century that this genre was recognized as a distinctive style and became well known and sought after by collectors.[8] By that time, much of the art was called "ledger art." (The term "ledger" or "ledgerbook" comes from the fact that merchant and army ledgers were a ready and desirable source of paper for the Indians, particularly after 1876.) However, ledger art largely represented a carryover of the old pictographic style to new materials. What had been produced on hide and wood was now produced on paper and cloth. What had been drawn with charcoal sticks and colored with earthen or vegetable-based pigments was now drawn with pencil and pen and colored with crayon, ink, or watercolor. Kicking Bear's work reflects this Indian adaptation to new materials.

Before analyzing Kicking Bear's painting, it may be helpful to explain the U.S. Army's version of the events depicted in the painting. The documentary account provides a useful comparison and contrast with Kicking Bear's pictorial record. On June 25, 1876, Lt. Col. George Custer knew that he was approaching a long sought Lakota village. Some time after noon, he split his U.S. Seventh Cavalry regiment into detachments in order to better scout and envelop the village. Custer did this as a direct result of what he perceived to be indications that his movement had been discovered. This would mean that the warrior forces might be alerted and waiting and that the main village might now decamp in all directions. Such a response would frustrate the Army's goal in the campaign, for a dispersed "hostile" force would be impossible to contain and "bring in."

Major Marcus A. Reno was assigned a battalion consisting of Companies A, H, and M, giving him something over 130 soldiers and scouts. Captain Frederick Benteen received three companies as well, about the same strength, but he was dispatched on a scout to the left. Benteen's movement was probably in compliance with the orders of Custer's superior, Alfred H. Terry, to "constantly feel to his left."[9] Custer himself took five companies, C, E, F, I, and L, giving him a battalion of about 215 men. Additional soldiers were assigned to guard the pack train. This rearguard escort required so many men that it was the second largest concentration of Seventh Cavalry troops.

Towards mid-afternoon, Reno was ordered to "attack afterwards" what appeared to be a fleeing encampment. This would take him to the south end of the village. Reno also was told, according to several witnesses, that he would be "supported by the whole outfit." However, the "whole outfit" was now divided into four disparate parts. Custer's battalion was the sole unit in supporting range of Reno's force.

If we assume that Reno understood the tactical doctrine of the day, Reno would have expected that his object was to charge the enemy's formation and, at the right moment, withdraw back onto the supporting force. The Army leadership had practiced and developed this maneuver during the four brutal years of the American Civil War [1861-1865].[10] It was generally accepted that cavalry, especially light cavalry, had no staying power. Shock, surprise, speed were then, as now, the constants of cavalry fighting. Experienced officers knew when it was the right time to return over the ground of the charge in order to regroup under the protection of the supporting force. On the other hand, since

Reno's orders were to "attack afterward," it appears that Custer may have had a second tactical maneuver in mind: a pursuit. If so, Reno's troopers would simply follow the fleeing Indians until the possibility of counterattack became evident. The pursuing force was then to deploy into skirmish line formation pending the arrival of the supporting force.[11] Either option would have required that Custer remain in supporting distance of Reno.

In this author's interpretation of events, Reno reached a point where he thought he had advanced far enough. He then went into skirmish line formation and waited for the anticipated "support by the whole outfit" that never came. Soon what has been variously described as a "dash," a "rout," a "charge," or a "retreat" was made out of the woods onto the flood plain, across the river, and up the bluffs on the east side. Eventually Reno's force was joined by Benteen's battalion and, later, by the pack train and its guards. By that time, the Indians were heading north, downriver, to defeat Custer in a separate fight. With that information as a background, let us now turn to the painting and see what Kicking Bear was trying to say about the battle.

Interpreted properly, Kicking Bear's painting can be used to gain further insight into the Reno fight. As we move around the painting, we should be able to find indications of events in which Kicking Bear personally participated. We should be able to verify some Indian oral testimony by use of the artistic testimony. However, this will require that we understand how the stylized and conventionalized language of pictographic art was used to portray various actions. It is also necessary to mention that the pictographic style was so highly personal that some of the details could only be explained by the artist. The following analysis will try to avoid reading meanings into any part of the painting that only Kicking Bear could have interpreted.

Before proceeding to the structure of the painting, it might be best to deal with some of the less significant points. Several details at the margins or edges are interesting. In the lower right corner are four women pointing to the left side of the picture. One of the women is holding what appears to be either a U. S. flag of a cavalry guidon. The cavalry guidons (unit markers) used at the troop or company level at this time were the same colors as the flag of the United States. However, the guidons were simply banners with a "swallow tail," while the women appear to be pointing to a full rectangle of cloth. Either way, the women seem to be emphasizing that a great defeat has taken place, whether that of

Little Big Horn, by Kicking Bear, 1898. *Southwest Museum, Los Angeles, California.*

Reno's detachment (represented by a guidon) or the entire U.S. Army's (represented by the national flag).

In another marginal area (at the bottom edge) are hoof prints. This is a conventional pictographic technique for showing movement to or from an area. Yet these hoof prints go toward the village, contrary to the way the action is flowing. This author's supposition is that these tracks represent the return of the warriors to the village at the end of the fighting. In a third marginal area (the left edge), we see another pictographic convention in the form of a row of muzzle blasts, which indicate rifle fire.

Another interesting detail is the outlines of figures that were never painted. Kicking Bear drew a total of seventy-seven—twenty-nine Indians and forty-eight cavalrymen—full, colored figures. There are fourteen Indian dead including an Arikara [Sahnish] Indian Army scout killed by Kicking Bear. But there are also thirteen or fifteen figures that are merely outlined. (The exact count of the outlined figures depends on which limbs go with which figures.) One can be seen in the lower center, and the remainder are in the upper left hand corner in the depiction of Custer's "Last Stand." Cobb's label stated that the empty outlined figures represented "spirits escaping from bodies and the still dying." If they represent departing spirits, however, there likely would be more of them. Also, a close examination of several completed figures reveals that making such an outline was apparently Kicking Bear's preliminary step before he finished by watercoloring the figure. An empty outline probably means that Kicking Bear changed his mind about the arrangement of some figures and abandoned them. The single unfinished figure in the lower center seems to confirm this. There is also a finished, colored figure lying slightly off the outline, as if Kicking Bear decided to shift the location a bit. Another explanation for the outlined figures may be that he simply didn't finish them.

In examining the structure of the painting, perhaps the first thing many readers will observe is that the general sense of movement seems to be from right to left (see figure 1). Several experts have identified this orientation as standard in Indian pictographic art.[12] However, this right to left motion can be disorienting to those unaccustomed to it. In most of the cultures of the "Western" or European-derived world, things are read from left to right. This is true whether reading words on a page or the sequence of events in a picture. This cultural difference may be one reason why Indian depictions of historic events have often been misunderstood.

It is useful to divide the painting into several sections based on what appears to be the logical and artistic flow of action (see figure 2). It would be reasonable to expect that since Kicking Bear participated in two separate actions on June 25—one against Reno and the other against Custer—there would be at least two distinct narrative segments in the painting. In fact, it is possible to distinguish five distinct sections. The first is a village area in the lower right; the second is a central group of four Indians about whom all the action seems to swirl; the third is a representation on the left of the famous "Last Stand" made by Custer's battalion; the fourth is a section of figures flowing diagonally across the canvas (labeled "the charge" in figure 2); and the fifth is a section composed of two rows of figures along the top of the canvas (labeled "skirmish lines" in figure 2).

Each of these five areas represents a separate event or situation. This technique of including several events or situations in a single work is not unusual in this Indian art style. (In fact, European artists engaged in this practice as late as the Renaissance.) For whatever reason, it seemed important to many Indian artists to include everything important within the same canvas. Another

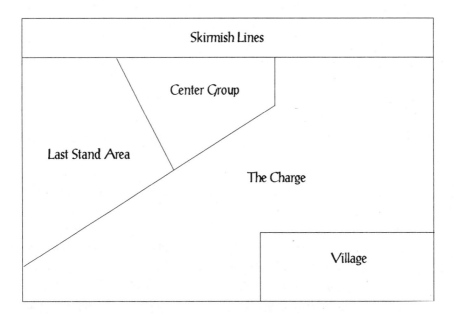

Figure 1: This graphic depicts the five major areas of Kicking Bear's painting. With the exception of the hoof print markings at the bottom center, all movement in this painting, as in so many pictographic artworks, is from right to left. *Submitted by author; digitized by Theodore P. Savas*

Indian artist of this battle, a Crow scout named White Swan, produced several works which also include multiple events.[13]

The village depicted in the first section, is one of the most unusual areas of the painting. It alone is free of the living and dead intermingled throughout the painting. This reflects the actual situation in the Indian village on the day of the Battle of the Little Bighorn. According to those who were in the village that day, it was at peace, unprepared for an attack. Kicking Bear's representation testifies to this. Other pictographic artworks of this village, such as those by Red Horse and White Swan, do the same.[14] At the time the battle began, it was a village preparing to move, yet one still observing mourning for the warriors lost in a battle with George Crook's column of troops on Rosebud Creek a week earlier. (It was a small group of such mourners that Custer's scouts jumped east of the village at what is now known as the "Lone Tipi/Tepee" in battle literature.)

The encampment was larger than most, having recently grown from over 800 lodges to around 2,000.[15] There were several circles, one for each of the Lakota and Cheyenne bands, such as the Lakota's Oglala, Minneconjou, etc. Kicking Bear represents them all with a single circle, however. Although he has compressed the circle into a flattened oval, this is not necessarily inaccurate—the circles were seldom perfectly round.

A village in wartime would have been filled with the dust of hundreds of ponies being prepared for the fight and with smoke from several hundred lodge fires. There would also be, amid the mass of multicolored lodges, meat drying racks, horse lines, weapons stands, and all the other accoutrements of a nomadic life on the Plains. However, Kicking Bear's village appears barren, except for the presence of a cooking post and several dogs playing about. He shows an empty village because, as word of the attack by Reno's battalion in the valley spread, the women, children, and elderly evacuated the lodges. Notice the pictographic footprints running throughout the tepees. These probably represent a hasty departure. The author contends that the position of this village in the painting accurately reflects the location of the encampment relative to the "Last Stand" area of Custer's battalion. In several other pictographic paintings, the encampment is in this same relative location. There has been a longstanding dispute about the precise location of the village. This author is convinced, from Indian testimony and such Indian artwork as Kicking Bear's, that the north end of the village was opposite the point where Medicine Tail Coulee—a "coulee" is a shallow ravine or stream bed—emptied into the Bighorn River. For too long, the village has been placed with its center opposite the coulee.

Part of Custer's battalion went down Medicine Tail Coulee to the river. They were presumably ordered to do so based on what Custer observed of the main encampment from Weir Point, a vantage point on the high ground to the east. Apparently Custer could see from there that the coulee was opposite the village's north end. Custer would have been aware that, as shown in Kicking Bear's painting, the village was being evacuated as a result of Reno's attack. By moving to a point sufficiently north, he could deploy a force between the noncombatants fleeing the village and the warriors engaging Reno to the south. Getting between the warriors and the noncombatants was a proven tactic in Indian warfare, one that usually brought the fighting to an end. Custer's view from Weir Point apparently convinced him that such an opportunity presented itself. In this light, his decision to deploy further north and downriver, away from Reno, makes sense.

The central group, the second section, is an interesting composition (see figure 3). Its members stand calmly while all the battle action seems to flow around them. According to the inscriptions, the men are Sitting Bull (Tatanka-Iy-otanka), Rain-In-The-Face ("Rainy Face" on the map), Crazy Horse (Tashunca-Witco), and Kicking Bear himself. One would assume that Kicking Bear would have supervised the labeling of the four figures. However, as will soon be seen, someone obviously made a mistake when labeling two of the figures. This raises the important possibility that other mistakes were made, either in the structure of the painting or in the labeling of the figures.

Sitting Bull, on the left, is shown facing the viewer. Kicking Bear painted him holding two rifles in his right hand and a bow and arrows in his left, and dressed in a red fringed shirt with blue and white beadwork, two coup feathers, blue breechcloth, and yellow leggings. Sitting Bear would seem to be a natural choice for inclusion in the painting. However, readers should be aware that there are conflicts in the Indian testimonies about if, where, or how Sitting Bull was involved in the battle. This cannot be solved here. This author tends to believe that, regardless of where he was at the time of the battle, Kicking Bear would have been sure to include Sitting Bull since he and Kicking Bear were among the last of the stronghearted "traditionals" to resist white domination. It does seem odd that Kicking Bear would portray his leader, Sitting Bull, holding captured weapons. Students of the battle know that Sitting Bull warned his

Figure 2: The Central Group. *Southwest Museum, LA*

people not to strip the enemy dead or to take anything from them, as that would ruin their victory. Probably only Kicking Bear himself could have explained why these the Army weapons were included in a representation of Sitting Bull. The second figure from the left is labeled "Rainy Face" (Rain-In-The-Face). But is it? Evidence points to the fact that

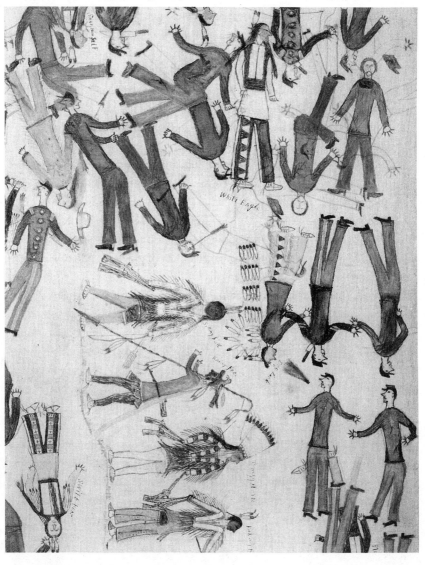

the supposed Rain-In-The-Face is labeled erroneously. In fact, all available evidence suggests that the second figure is in fact Crazy Horse. Many of the known details about Crazy Horse can be found in Stephen E. Ambrose's *Crazy Horse and Custer: The Parallel Lives of Two American Warriors*, and in Mari Sandoz's *Crazy Horse: The Strange Man of the Oglalas*. Both books draw on most of the major primary sources.

The hair on the painting's Rain-In-The-Face is braided, with something hanging before his left ear and what appears to be a hawk cresting his head. Both Ambrose and Sandoz, and indeed all other sources seen by this author, describe Crazy Horse with braided hair, a small rock tied over his left ear, and often adorned with a preserved hawk as a head decoration. According to Ambrose, Crazy Horse's battle dress was as follows: "His hair was light and long . . . [He] almost always wore in it braids. . . . [G]oing into battle [he] never wore more than a breechcloth and leggings, a single hawk feather in his hair, his ever present small stone behind his ear and another stone under his left arm." Mari Sandoz, in describing Crazy Horse at the Fetterman Fight in 1866, wrote, "The red backed Hawk was on his head, behind his ear hung the little stone, and on his cheek sat the white lightning streak."[16] The second figure also appears to have a white or light paint streak down the left side of his face, and there are white markings on what are either red-tinted leggings or bare legs painted red. Either the paint streak on the face or the leggings markings could be the type of "white lightning streak" associated with Crazy Horse.

Kicking Bear's Rain-In-The Face is also shown wearing an unidentifiable military society's sash, which flows down the figure's back from around his neck or shoulder. (The sash is barely perceptible due to fading.) The figure is armed with a rifle (at his waist) and holds a characteristically crooked "leaders'" lance. Such lances were used in Plains warrior societies to designate permanent or temporary leaders of war parties or similar groups. Historians Ambrose and Sandoz note that Crazy Horse and a man named He Dog were honored by being permitted to bear the two lances of the Crow Owners warrior society, "the two lances of the Oglalas, the two lances that had been with the people longer than any man could remember."[17]

While there are many descriptions of Crazy Horse, there are few of Rain-In-The-Face. However, Rain-In-The Face can only be the third figure from the left, the one labeled "Crazy Horse." This third figure wears a blue fringed shirt with white and blue beadwork and a conical feather bonnet. His hair is loose flowing from the back of the bonnet, and he appears to have a piece of cloth or hide wrapped around his neck.

The fourth and last figure from the left is Kicking Bear himself. He is shown wearing a green fringed shirt, black breech cloth, yellow leggings, two coup feathers, and carrying two captured weapons in his right hand and a scalp stick in his left. Kicking Bear is shown pointing to a prone figure on his left who represents an Arikara Army scout he slew in battle. Just above the scout's waist is a dark conical shape, a pictographic convention representing a weapon firing; this seems to show that Kicking Bear shot the man with a gun. The hatched lines encircling the scout were another device that Kicking Bear used to indicate footprints. The dead scout is labeled only "Ree [Arikara] with Soldiers." However, another famous Lakota artist, Amos Bad Heart Bull, drew a pictograph of the individual combat in which the scout was slain. The Arikara's name is known to be Little Brave, and he was killed by Kicking Bear as Reno's troops withdrew to the east side of the Little Bighorn River and up the hillside.[18]

In the picture's caption, Cobb wrote that "Kicking Bear leaves blank the space where Gall, as head chief, should be shown." However, there does not appear to be any blank space in this grouping. Kicking Bear might conceivably have drawn himself closer to his victim and placed Gall between himself and the third figure. But other than that, there does not seem to be any space in which Gall could have been placed. Perhaps the remark about Gall is another example of romanticizing by Cobb or his source.[19]

Kicking Bear included thirteen Lakota dead in the painting (see figure 4). All of them are labeled by name, making the painting a valuable document in identifying some of the Indian casualties.[20] Six of the Lakota depicted in Kicking Bear's painting died in the actions against Marcus Reno's men on June 25 and 26. The death sites of the Indian dead in the Reno fight were often remembered later, and some were even marked with rock piles as monuments. Hardorff mentions such a marker for the man named Long Road, for example.[21] The other seven identified Lakota casualties were killed in the fight with Custer's forces. While there is available Indian testimony about Indian deaths in the Custer fight, much of that information is non-specific (describing the dead only as "a Lakota," "wearing a feathered bonnet," etc.). Of the seven who fell fighting Custer, the death sites of only two are known. Black White Man was severely wounded on the west slope of what is known as Last Stand or Custer Hill, just beneath the crest. He died on June 27 and was buried on Wood Louse

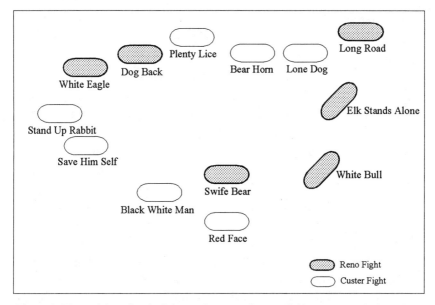

Figure 3: The position of each slain warrior according to Kicking Bear's painting. These locations do not appear to coincide with eyewitness testimony. For example, White Eagle and Dog Back were killed around Reno's position, yet Kicking Bear placed them around the Last Stand area. He showed multiple locations by type (Calhoun and Reno defensive lines) with a single pictographic composition, thus creating what appears to be a discrepancy. *Submitted by author; digitized by Theodore P. Savas.*

Creek.[22] Bear Horn was killed about halfway down the slope of Battle Ridge, between the points called Custer Hill and Calhoun Hill.[23]

As noted earlier, Kicking Bear was an enthusiastic participant in the fight with Reno's troops on June 25. He was in the fighting from the beginning, defending the village. He can later be placed in the attack on Reno on the east side of the river, for he killed the Arikara scout there. He took part in the battle against Custer's forces as well, but not as extensively as in the contest with Reno's men. We can make certain assumptions as a result of this information. One is that Kicking Bear would probably place greater emphasis on the Reno fight. We might expect that most of the events in the painting relate to that and not the battle with Custer's men. A second assumption is that Kicking Bear clearly understood that there were two separate and distinct combats, one with Reno's detachment and one with Custer's.

A third section of the painting, the Custer fight or Last Stand section, is on the left. There is good reason to give it this identification. The dead are tightly clustered there, and Custer's body is labeled. Also, the body of Black White Man, who is known to have died on Last Stand Hill, is in the lower right of this section. Strangely, the bodies of White Eagle and Dog Back, who definitely died in the Reno fight and not the Custer fight, are immediately above, if not in, the Last Stand section.

The section of men, living and dead, running diagonally across the picture is a fourth section. This section clearly represents the Reno fight. It begins, using pictographic conventions, on the right, just above the village. Swift Bear and White Bull, who were among the first to fall in Reno's initial attack, are shown in the center of the diagonal section, not far from the village.

The fifth section of Kicking Bear's painting consists of the two horizontal lines of fallen soldiers and Indians across the top of the painting. This section is the most puzzling. At first glance it appears to be a skirmish line. If so, it may represent the skirmish lines used in Reno in his attack on the village. On the other hand, we know that James Calhoun's L Company, one of the companies that fought with Custer, fought in a skirmish line formation. It would be easier to assume that the horizontal section represents the Reno fight in some way. That would explain the presence of White Eagle's and Dog Back's bodies above the Last Stand on the far left. The body of Long Road is on the extreme right, and he is also known to have died fighting Reno's men. However, the bodies of Plenty Lice, Bear Horn, and Long Dog are in the same line, and all oral testimony points to the last three as having been killed in the Custer fight.

Could Kicking Bear have made an error in the composition of the painting? Are more of the figures simply mislabeled? Actually, it could simply be that the top section with its two rows of soldiers may serve a dual use: it may represent events at both the Reno-Benteen defensive site and the positions of Custer's men on Battle Ridge. It might also be that the top section represents some way of grouping various events that took place on the east side of the river, or it might be an example of the "conceptual" perspective that non-Western cultures have often favored over "visual" perspective.

If we combine oral testimony, a knowledge of pictographic conventions, and some surmise, here is what Kicking Bear's picture may be telling us (see figure 5). Both Elk Stands Alone and White Eagle are known to have been killed on the east side of the river, while chasing Reno's men uphill. Dog Back and Long Road were both killed approaching Reno's final defensive lines, but they were killed on opposite ends of Reno's defensive perimeter. Bear Hunt is known to have been killed attacking a defensive line near, but not on, the site of the Last Stand. It is not known exactly where Plenty Lice and Long Dog were killed, but the painting seems to suggest that it was in a similar area, perhaps even near Bear Horn. Kicking Bear placed Black White Man in a position that accords with oral testimony. There is no such testimony regarding the places where Red Face, Stand Up Rabbit, and Saves Him Self [sic] died. However, if Kicking Bear depicted Red Face in a position relative to that of Black White Man, Red Face was killed down the slope from Black White Man. Perhaps Red Face died in the now-famous "Deep Coulee" where at least two unnamed Lakota warriors' bodies were seen after the fighting. By the same logic, Stand Up Rabbit and Saves Him Self must also have died in the Last Stand area. The author believes that Kicking Bear's painting locates several previously unknown death sites. Perhaps Frederic Remington expected a painting showing how George Custer died. Had he claimed his purchase, he would have instead received a representation of where (and how) thirteen Lakota warriors died protecting their homes and families.

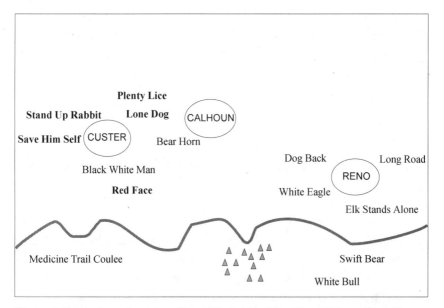

Figure 4: Death sites of warriors (Stand Up Rabbit, Save Himself, Long Dog, Plenty Lice, and Red Face) identified here for the first time are in **bold** text. They are based on Kicking Bear's painting and eyewitness testimony. Many survivors talked of slain warriors in the Last Stand area, but no one knew their names. According to author Rod Thomas, he is "certain that they fell as depicted" above. *Submitted by author; digitized by Theodore P. Savas.*

Kicking Bear's painting is, first and foremost, about Indians. Kicking Bear's painting apparently does not provide us with any new information or insights into why the U.S. Seventh Cavalry met disaster at the Little Bighorn. It does, however, provide us with a means of recovering the understandings and memories of a warrior who fought the Battle of the Little Bighorn. And in that way such paintings can increase our knowledge of the battle.

Helen Blish, in her seminal work on American Indian pictographic art, challenged us thusly: "For matters of comparison, not only from the point of view of art but also from the point of view of historical record as such, the interpretations of White Bird and Red Horse, with those of Bad Heart Bull, form a source group that should possess some real value."[24] Had she seen the Kicking Bear painting, perhaps she would have included it as one of her chief examples.

As demonstrated here, it is possible to make several sound conclusions from this art form regarding the historical events they portray. Previous analytical work using pictographic paintings did not receive much attention. Hopefully, this article will spur further analysis of such works. It is possible to compare white and Indian testimony with pictographic art of the Reno fight and find that the sources complement one another. Could we not, then, take other Indian testimony and art work and do the same in analyzing Custer's fight? I feel certain that we can do this and be on safe ground historically with our conclusions.

NOTES

1. Helen Blish, *A Pictographic History of the Oglala Sioux* (Lincoln: University of Nebraska Press, 1967), 217-218.

2. Web site for Rock Creek Publishing Group, Inc., Bethesda, Maryland, 1997 (http://www.rcpub.com/dir/). Accessed April 3, 1998.

3. Several discussions with Kim Waters, head of the Braun Research Library, Southwest Museum, indicated that there is no information on the painting's provenance other than what is on the label that Cobb affixed to the frame.

4. A typically cursory comment on Kicking Bear's painting may be found in Margot Liberty, editor, "Last Ghastly Moments at The Little Big Horn," *American Heritage*, 17, no. 3, (April 1966), 14-21, 72-73. Kicking Bear's painting is reproduced on pp. 16-17 of

this article. The caption on p. 17 quotes some of the painting's label directly but without citing the source.

5. The author believes that this is the first time the painting's label had been published in its entirety. It is interesting to read in it the popular beliefs of Cobb's time about Indians, soldiers, and the particulars of the Little Bighorn fight.

6. E. A. Brininstool, *Troopers with Custer: Historic Incidents of the Battle of the Little Big Horn* (Mechanicsburg: Stackpole Books, 1994).

7. George Catlin, George, *Letters and Notes on the Manners, Customs, and Conditions of the North American Indians* (New York: Dover Press, 1973).

8. Janet Berlo, *The Early Days of Native American Art History: The Politics of Scholarship and Collecting* (Seattle: The University of Washington Press, 1993).

9. *Report of the Secretary of War, 1876*, Volume I, 44th Cong., 2nd sess., Ex. Doc. 1, Part 2, 462.

10. *Cavalry Tactics: United States Army Assimilated to the Tactics of Infantry and Artillery* (New York: D. Appleton and Company, 1876). This was the official tactics manual in effect for the period 1873-1887. General Orders Number 6 is dated July 17, 1873, despite the 1876 publication date of the volume.

11. The author has reviewed U. S. Army Cavalry doctrine from 1841 to the present. The deliberate charge and the pursuit remain viable tactical and operational maneuvers. Custer may have intended Reno to be part of a third type of tactical maneuver, that being the classic maneuver today termed the "hammer and anvil" tactic. In this third option, one force was to immobilize the enemy while the other struck. This would have required the "anvil," i.e., Reno's detachment, to be larger than the force that Custer assigned him.

12. Candace S. Greene, "Women, Bison, and Coup: A Structural Analysis of Cheyenne Pictographic Art" (Ph. D. diss., University of Oklahoma, 1985).

13. Douglas E. Bradley, cataloger, *White Swan: Crow Indian Warrior and Painter* (Notre Dame, Indiana: The Snite Museum of Art, University of Notre Dame, 1991).

14. Document collection, catalogue number 2367-A, National Anthropological Archives, Smithsonian Institute, Washington, D. C. There are forty-two pictographs and one map drawn by Red Horse in this collection. They have been used so many times that the originals have been withdrawn from public use. Catalogue numbers 406, 407, 408, United States Military Academy Museum, West Point, New York. Blish, *Pictographic History of the Oglala Sioux*, pp. 19, 56-57.

15. John S. Gray, *The Centennial Campaign: The Sioux War of 1876* (Fort Collins, Colorado: Old Army Press, 1976. Every serious student of the campaign since 1976 has utilized Gray's analysis of the village's numbers, though not necessarily his analysis of

its area. The village's placement, length, width, and shape are still debated by scholars. This encampment deserves more serious study; obviously what (and what was not) happening within it had a significant influence on the Reno fight.

16. Steven E. Ambrose, *Crazy Horse and Custer: The Parallel Lives of Two American Warriors* (New York: Penguin Books, 1986), 159; Mari Sandoz, *Crazy Horse: The Strange Man of the Oglalas* (Lincoln: Bison Books, University of Nebraska Press, 1992), 198.

17. Ambrose, *Crazy Horse and Custer*, 137; Sandoz, *Crazy Horse,* 237.

18. Blish, *Pictographic History of the Oglala Sioux*, figure 161 on p. 247.

19. In a recent book about the battle, Robert Nightengale included a photograph of a painting similar to the one examined here. In fact, it looks as if it could have been another version painted by Kicking Bear. In Nightengale's illustration there are only three standing figures in the central group, and there actually is a space between Sitting Bull and Rain-In-The-Face. Is it a preliminary study done by Kicking Bear? Attempts to contact the author have failed, and the publisher has not been helpful in providing information on the painting's location. I have sent copies to the staff of the Southwest Museum, Father Peter Powell, and several other scholars, all of whom state they have never seen the painting in Nightendale's book. Until the painting shown in his book is properly identified, it can only be assumed that Kicking Bear produced only one painting. For now, Cobb's label can still not be reconciled with what can be seen in the painting he possessed. Robert Nightengale, *Little Big Horn* (Edina: Far West Publishing, 1996), 140.

20. Plains Indians routinely had three names and often more. If they were known to other bands of the same tribe or other tribes, they would have be known by even more names among those other bands. There are nine figures that have differing names depending upon the sources consulted. The label names are listed here, with alternate English language names of each man included in parenthesis: (1) Stand Up Rabbit (Young Skunk on most battle casualty lists); (2) Save Him Self [sic] (Yellow Hair, Bad Yellow Hair, Bad Light Hair, usually Bad Yellow Hair on lists); (3) Black White Man (Black Wasichu); (4) Dog Back (Backbone of Dog, Dog's Backbone); (5) Plenty Lice (Many Lice on most lists); (6) Bear Horn (Bear on casualty lists); (7) Long Road (Eagle Hat, Thunder Shield); (8) One Dog (Lone Dog); and (9) Elk Standing Alone (Elk Stands Alone, Elk Stands Above, Elk Stands On Top, Elk, High Elk; Elk Standing on casualty lists). These name differences become important when trying to research individual Indian, their actions, and in this case, their deaths. Since "Stand Up Rabbit" and "Save Him Self" do not appear on any other references to the Indian dead, historian Richard

Hardorff concluded these were nicknames for Young Skunk and Bad Yellow Hair. Richard G. Hardorff, *Hokahey! A Good Day to Die! The Indian Casualties of the Custer Fight*. (Spokane: The Arthur H. Clark Company, 1993), 132-133.

21. Ibid., 90-91.

22. Ibid., 79.

23. Ibid., 65.

24. Blish, *Pictographic History of the Oglala Sioux*, 20.

Cheyenne Dog Soldiers

A Ledgerbook History
of Coups and Combats

Courtesy of the Colorado Historical Society and the
University Press of Colorado

*C*heyenne Dog Soldiers: A Ledgerbook History of Coups and Combats is
the result of an important collaborative project of the Colorado
Historical Society and the University Press of Colorado. The work successfully
combines Western documentary history, ethno-history, and Indian art history.
The authors of *Cheyenne Dog Soldiers* (Niwot: Colorado Historical Society and
the University Press of Colorado, 1997) are Jean Afton, David Fridtjof Halaas,
and Andrew E. Masich, with Richard N. Ellis.

A general description of the book, which includes a definition of the
"ledgerbook style" of art, appears in the lead book review of this issue. Most of
the information below is taken from the authors' commentaries. The names of
the warriors used in the book were derived from their name glyphs, small
symbols placed over the warriors' heads in most of the drawings. The
photographs are provided courtesy of their owner, the Colorado Historical
Society.

Cheyenne Dog Soldiers is an important book which substantially adds to
our understanding of Indian art history.

*   *   *

Plate 37:

"The Bow Lance Protects the Brave Warrior"
by Red Lance

In this image, Red Lance is depicted firing three shots at a fleeing soldier. Eyes wide in terror, the soldier extends his hat in a gesture of submission. Red Lance will evidently pursue his quarry up to a line of soldiers (indicated by the vertical line of rifle muzzle bursts on the left). However, the warrior's bow lance, a sacred weapon often associated with the Kit Fox military order, together with other sacred accoutrements, protects him from harm. Red Lance's drawings are typically bold and emphatic.

*   *   *

Plate 48:

"Lanced Between the Eyes"
by Lean Bear, Feathered Bear, and Bear Man

This drawing by several artists depicts White Face Bull lancing a dismounted trooper, this despite the passage of bullets over the warrior's head. The trooper is drawn in sufficient detail to determine his rank as a noncommissioned soldier (by the trouser stripe) and to identify the model numbers of his weapons and gear, including the model 1859 McClellan horse equipment. The authors believe that this scene may depict the killing of one of fifteen solders at a fight at Julesburg, Colorado, January 7, 1865.

* * *

Plate 61:

"Capturing the Herd"
by Knows His Gun

Knows His Gun was unusual in that he often portrayed himself in a three-quarter view versus the more traditional profile view. In addition, the proud pose and visible energy of his horses are unique. The warrior is shown conducting what appears to be a one-man horse raid, armed only with a shield and a coup stick. (A coup stick was used for touching an enemy, an act considered the ultimate act of bravery.)

*   *   *

Plate 63:

"Catching an Army Horse"
by Warrior Z

"Warrior Z" is the name given to an artist unidentified by a name glyph. The horse equipment is shown in intricate detail in this image, down to the clubbed tail of the Dog Soldier's horse and the 1859 picket pin still barely restraining the Army mount. The authors identify the scene with a February 4, 1865, raid at Mud Springs Station, Colorado.

*   *   *

Plate 81:

"A Running Fight"
by Bear Man

Bear Man was one of the most accomplished Dog Soldier artists, as he demonstrates in this depiction of the great warrior Whirlwind (one of the few persons in the book who can be identified historically). The event may be the same one apparently portrayed in Plate 48, the riding down of fifteen troops at Julesburg, Colorado, on January 7, 1865.

Bear Man's drawings give a unique grace to horses in motion. Note that the greatcoat-clad soldier is riding a spotted Appaloosa horse, an Indian breed.

*   *   *

Interview

A Conversation with Gerald K. Keenan
(author of *Encyclopedia of the Indian Wars*)

Interviewed by Michael A. Hughes

Gerald K. Keenan's recent *Encyclopedia of the Indian Wars, 1492-1890* (Santa Barbara: ABC-CLIO, 1997) is the first published effort to provide a comprehensive reference work on the Indian wars within what is now the continental United States. His previous works include *The Wagon Box Fight* (various publishers and editions) and *Hostiles and Horse Soldiers: Indian Battles and Campaigns in the West,* with Lonnie J. White (Boulder,1972). Mr. Kennan is also an experienced editor of Indian wars-related manuscripts, and it was in that capacity he came to know many of the experts in the field personally. For these reasons, an interview with "Jerry" Keenan seemed a natural fit for the premier issue of *Journal of the Indian Wars*.

* * *

MAH: What inspired you to write Encyclopedia of the Indian Wars?

JK: The fact that nothing like it had been attempted. The Indian wars are a long and important part of American history. But no one had ever provided a general reference that could be used by students and readers.

MAH: Why are the Indian wars significant, and why should they be studied?

JK: The Indian wars were one way, right or wrong, that the growth of the young United States became possible. It sounds harsh to say this, but the wars did resolve a lot of conflicts between competing claims to the land. It often resolved them tragically and regrettably, but it did resolve them. And you also have to remember that in many cases the Indian wars weren't just conflicts between Indians and whites. Many times they were tied to the competition between rival European countries for North America. I would say study them because, good or bad, they're an essential part of American history. I would also say that perhaps in studying them we can resolve to see some good come, somehow, out of the wrongs done.

MAH: Were there any surprises for you in researching your book?

JK: Yes, learning about the wars in the East, especially in the Southeast and New England, was a revelation to me. I had only a vague perception of what happened there before this. The fierceness and the scale of the warfare there—in things like King Philip's [Metacom's] War, or Pontiac's "Rebellion," or the French and Indian Wars, went far beyond anything out West. And, although they're even more overlooked, some of the battles fought during the exploration period are even more amazing. . . .

MAH: Can you name some for us?

JK: Sure. The fight at Mabila, during De Soto's expedition, in 1540, was a huge affair. Good estimates place Indian casualties at 2,500. George Bancroft called Mabila "the greatest Indian battle ever fought within the United States." Yet, who has heard about it or even studied it?

MAH: That is surprising! What particular challenges or disappointments did you face in researching and writing the encyclopedia?

JK: The biggest challenge was deciding what to include and what had to be left out. This study encompasses events going all the way from 1492 to 1890. It was impossible in the pages available to cover everything that should be covered. In the end, it came down to deciding what was not just interesting, but what was critical. The biggest disappointment grew out of this problem, because I originally foresaw the book as a two-volume work. But the press decided to go with one volume.

MAH: You're considered the authority on the Wagon Box Fight. . . .

JK: Well, I'm flattered to be called "the authority" on the fight.

MAH: Can you provide us a bit of background on this incident?

JK: Sure. The Wagon Box Fight occurred in the Bozeman Trail or Red Cloud's War. In 1863, the Bozeman Trail was blazed through the Powder River country, a prime hunting ground of the Lakota Sioux and the Northern Cheyenne. The Army's construction of three forts along the trail in 1866 was considered a hostile act by the tribes, who replied with a series of attacks on the posts. On August 2, 1867, the Lakota attacked a party of men cutting wood near one of these forts, Fort Phil Kearny. The woodcutters formed a circle of wagon beds ("boxes") for defense. The defenders had recently been issued breech-loading rifles, which could be loaded more quickly and required less exposure to enemy fire while loading, than their previous muzzle-loading rifles. They managed to hold off the Indian attacks.

MAH: How did you get interested in this particular engagement?

JK: I became intrigued when J. W. Vaughan (author of *With Crook at the Rosebud*, *The Battle of Platte Bridge*, and *Indian Fights: New Facts on Seven Encounters*) told me that no one had really explored the battle and that someone should write about it. Vaughn was the first person to combine the use of metal detectors with material from library shelves to reconstruct a picture of what had happened at various battles. Why he didn't write on the Wagon Box Fight and Fort Phil Kearny himself, I don't know. I began by just by writing a paper and was pleased when the Fort Phil Kearny–Bozeman Trail Association felt that it was worth publishing as a monograph.

MAH: Yes, it is a great study. You later republished it yourself?

JK: Thanks. Yes, I did that when I set up a small press called Lightning Tree Press after I retired.

MAH: I heard through the grapevine you are still working on some aspect of the Wagon Box Fight?

JK: Right now I've working on a revision of the book, which takes some of the archaeological findings about the battle into account.

MAH: Was the significance of the Wagon Box Fight largely symbolic or did it alter events in some way?

JK: I've thought that one over for years. In terms of how it affected the situation of the Army in the Powder River country, including Fort Phil Kearny, it had no impact. As you know, the three Bozeman Trail forts were all abandoned soon afterwards. The victory did have an effect on the morale of the frontier army, though.

MAH: What about the effects of the event on weaponry?

JK: It's tempting to overemphasize the significance of breech-loading weapons. Certainly they played a key part in withstanding the attackers at the Wagon Box Fight. The fight demonstrated to the Army how much more effective breech-loaders were than muzzle-loaders. But there's a tendency to exaggerate the importance of such weapons in making an effective response to attacks. [George A.] Custer and his five companies were armed with breech-loaders at Little Bighorn in 1876, for example, and they were wiped out.

MAH: Haven't the odds and the Indian casualties at the Wagon Box Fight traditionally been exaggerated?

JK: Oh, yes. It makes for a much better story to say that there were 3,000 warriors against thirty-two defenders. The defenders were vastly outnumbered, but there's been a tendency to overdramatize the odds.

MAH: *If you were pressed to provide an approximate range for the number of Indians involved there, what would your answer be?*

JK: I would say about 800 to 1,000.

MAH: What about losses?

JK: Captain [James] Powell, the officer escorting the woodcutters, estimated that there were sixty Indian dead. All other estimates are off. Powell's is the most conservative, though still I believe somewhat exaggerated. I lean towards accepting his figure because Powell had considerable experience in the Civil War, and he was the most experienced man when it came to observing large numbers of men in action.

MAH: You mentioned that you were revising the book in light of archaeological discoveries. Can you share some of that with us?

JK: Sure. In 1997, the state of Wyoming published an archaeological survey containing the results of investigations in 1993 and 1994. Essentially, I'm working those findings into the book. They really won't alter significantly any conclusions in the book.

MAH: Did any new information come out from these investigations?

JK: Yes. The survey concluded that the corral was at the large stone marker on the field versus the pipe marker. That's what most of us have contended in recent years.

MAH: It must be gratifying to have that investigation verify your conclusions. What was the "pipe marker"?

JK: That was a marker put up by Walter Camp, a compiler of vast amounts of Plains Indian war documents and oral accounts in the decades immediately following the Indian wars. When I first visited it, you could go directly to it from the stone marker. Now you'd have to cross fences marking private land.

MAH: *You have written quite a few articles, and I've even seen "with Jerry Keenan" listed on a book on raising pedigree cats! What different sorts of things have you written?*

JK: I've written more book reviews than I can keep track of. And, as you mentioned, there are some articles, including several on the scout Yellowstone Kelly. . . .

MAH: *Wasn't one of those an award winner?*

JK: Yes, it was. It won the Western Heritage Award from the National Cowboy Hall of Fame. I got to visit your state, Oklahoma, to receive that award and got a steak dinner out of it as well!

MAH: *What else have you written?*

JK: I've also written, believe it or not, a contract novel, *The Battle of Horsetooth Mountain.* Oh, and after many years a manuscript on James Wilson's Union cavalry is about to be published by McFarland Press. I guess the moral of that study is "be persistent."

MAH: *What are your next projects?*

JK: I'm doing another book for ABC-CLIO, the publisher of my *Encyclopedia of the Indian Wars, 1492-1890.* This is also an encyclopedia, but the topic is the Spanish-American War and the Philippine Insurrection. Also, I'm about a third of the way through a manuscript on Yellowstone Kelly.

MAH: *Kelly had a fascinating life.*

JK: Yes, he did. He was an Army scout for General Nelson Miles in the late Sioux campaigns. After that he traveled to Alaska for a while, then was a captain of volunteers in the Philippines. He was also the agent at the San Carlos Apache Reservation from 1904 to 1908. That was when he was a friend of Theodore Roosevelt's.

MAH: Could you fill us in a bit more on Kelly's career as an Army scout?

JK: Kelly was living in the Judith Basin in Wyoming when he heard about the Custer debacle at Little Bighorn in June 1876. He went to offer his services to General Miles, who hired him immediately. Miles later made him chief scout of the Yellowstone District. While he was with Miles, he served in the wrap up campaigns against the Sioux, including Wolf Mountains, where Crazy Horse's Lakota band was defeated in Montana in 1877. Kelly and Miles had an interesting relationship. The two men were totally opposite in personality, but each found something he appreciated in the other.

MAH: Why was he called "Yellowstone" Kelly?

JK: I've never found a good explanation for it, and Kelly never said. He did spend a lot of time in the Yellowstone region. There's a nice story that he went around saying he wanted to find "yellow gold on the Yellowstone [River]," but I don't put much stock in it. The Indians had several names for him—"Lone Wolf" (for his propensity to spend time alone), "Little Man with Strong Heart" (I can't imagine why "Little Man" as he was nearly six feet tall), and "Man Who Never Lays Down His Gun."

MAH: How did you become involved in writing and editing?

JK: I began writing at home in the evenings while I was working in manufacturing. I wrote one novel that way, which was never published. I also kept working on a manuscript on Wilson's cavalry in the American Civil War. I got into editing "through the back door," so to speak. I was working for Bruce Publishing Company in Milwaukee, actually in cost and inventory control. While there, I did freelance writing—press releases, book jackets, that sort of thing. That gave me a good idea of how the publishing business worked. Later, after we moved to Colorado, I found myself in the right position to become the managing editor at Pruett Press in Boulder.

MAH: That is interesting. You're also a veteran. Were you ever under fire, and did any of your military experiences give you a greater understanding for the military history you write?

JK: I was a buck sergeant (a rank that no longer exists) in the One Hundred and Eleventh Marine Field Artillery, First Marine Division, in the Korean War. And, yes, there were times we were under fire, though it was long distance fire, counterbattery fire. Of course, that kind of experience helps in understanding the people you read about and write about. We came a century, or several centuries, after them, but I doubt the emotions you experience have changed. So to that extent, my service has helped me.

MAH: You're married to an author and editor, right?

JK: Yes, my wife, Carol Krismann, is, among other things, book review editor of the publication of the Colorado Library Association. She recently received a contract for her own book with ABC-CLIO, a reference guide to the history of American women in business.

MAH: Which reminds me . . . ABC-CLIO, the press that published your Encyclopedia of the Indian Wars, *is not a household name. It primarily publishes reference works, is that right?*

JK: Actually, ABC-CLIO is well established and pretty well known, but largely among librarians. As you say, ABC-CLIO concentrates on reference books.

MAH: What's your impression of your nearby neighbor, the University Press of Colorado? They seem to be quickly becoming a serious contender among the academic presses publishing Western and Indian history. Their new Cheyenne Dog Soldiers *[1997] looks as if it's going to be a model for artistic and ethno-historical research..*

JK: Yes, we're really proud here of what the press is doing. Luther Wilson, the press director, is supporting some very good projects.

MAH: What authors do you admire? And who have you learned from? Robert Utley's name has come up in conversations between us before. He would be, obviously I suppose, the "dean" of Indian wars authors.

JK: Absolutely. Utley's not only written more than anyone else, but he's done all of it authoritatively and well. I remember one incident that shows how others view him. We were at a Western History Association meeting together, in Omaha, I think it was, and an obviously talented graduate history student, maybe one with a new degree, but one who had no reason to be intimidated, found that Bob and his wife going to be in the audience. The man remarked that in his field [history] this was about like facing God.

MAH: And other authors?

JK: I've also gained an appreciation for Allan W. Eckert and James Alexander Thom, the biographers of Tecumseh. Also, though of course they're not Indian wars historians, I still like the work of Samuel Eliot Morrison, Bernard De Voto, Francis Parkman, and Barbara Tuchman. I realize that they are not all formally "historians," but writers like De Voto and Parkman and Tuchman have a way of making history come alive.

MAH: I noticed that in Eckert's work there are entire paragraphs of personal dialogue between characters. Are you comfortable with what appears to be speculative conversation in a non-fiction work?

JK: I've noticed that, too. All I can say is that there have been a few times that I've come across Eckert's sources, and those same conversations are found in his primary sources.

MAH: Is there any advice that you would give anyone hoping to learn to write history?

JK: Yes, read. Constantly. Especially read the work of historians who are not only good at their profession but also write well. Examine how they use words, how they put them together. It's a good source of inspiration. And keep writing. Writing is a skill that has to be practiced. And do more than one type of writing—just for the experience. I've mentioned earlier that I wrote a novel and I found that that helped my other writing as well. One reason that many historians don't have more of an audience is that they may be very good at researching and reaching conclusions, but that by itself isn't enough. They have to learn the craft of writing also.

MAH: Jerry, it has been a pleasure, and let me thank you for agreeing to be interviewed for Journal of the Indian Wars.

JK: You're welcome.

Features

The Story Behind Our Cover Art
and the Gilcrease Museum

Attack at Dawn by Charles Schreyvogel (1904. Oil on canvas, 34 x 46 in. /86 x 117 cm.), courtesy of the Gilcrease Museum, Tulsa, Oklahoma.

The 1876 Battle of the Little Bighorn is the subject of entire albums of images. By contrast, an earlier engagement involving George Custer, the 1868 battle or massacre on the Washita River, has been the inspiration for a mere handful of paintings. Among the most striking of these portrayals is Charles Schreyvogel's *Attack at Dawn*.

Schreyvogel was born in New York City in 1861 to a family of German immigrants. He received traditional academic art training in Munich. In 1893, a performance of Buffalo Bill's Wild West Show inspired the first of many journeys west to make sketches and to meet Indian wars veterans. The artist's notoriety today is partially derived from his rivalry with Frederic Remington. Journalistic acclaim for the 1903 *Custer's Demand* (also part of the Gilcrease Museum collection) led to violent protests by Remington that the painting contained inaccuracies in detail. Roundly defended against the charge by Elizabeth Bacon Custer and others, Schreyvogel won the debate. However, by the time Schreyvogel died of blood poisoning in 1912, it was already becoming apparent that history would judge Remington the greater artist.

Attack at Dawn includes the trademarks of Schreyvogel's work: theatrical drama, violent yet bloodless action, great care in the posing of horses, and near infallibility in the portrayal of costume, accoutrements, and weapons. While Schreyvogel achieved true portraiture in some earlier paintings, most faces are obscured in this one. There are some similarities between the poses in *Attack at Dawn* and Remington's *Battle of the Washita* (private collection). *Attack* is unusual in that it seemingly proceeds chronologically from left to right, from contact, through combat, to flight and pursuit. The mounted warrior's dash through the village probably never occurred since the horse herd was located too far from the tepees (lodges). Perhaps Schreyvogel was unable to obtain eye-witness testimonies for this effort. Or perhaps *Attack at Dawn* was intended to capture no more than the spirit of the event.

The Gilcrease Museum and the Whitney Gallery of Western Art of the Buffalo Bill Historical Center (Cody, Wyoming) are the major repositories of Schreyvogel's paintings. Regretfully, the sole slim work on Schreyvogel, James D. Horan's *The Life and Art of Charles Schreyvogel* (1969), has been long out of print. The most accessible information in print is found in William H. and William N. Goetzmann, *The West of the Imagination* (1986).

The Gilcrease Museum of Tulsa contains as many as 2,500 works related to the Indian wars. However, these are only a portion of the 7,500 works termed "Western" art. In all, the museum possesses 10,000 paintings, prints, and sculptures from the hands of more than 400 artists. Among its treasures, the Gilcrease preserves great collections of the representations of nineteenth century Indian life painted by frontier artists George Catlin and Alfred Jacob Miller. Of the most famous "cowboy and Indian" artists, Remington is represented by almost sixty works, and Russell by around ninety. The museum possesses six of Charles Schreyvogel's scarce paintings. There are also over 500 works by identifiable Indian artists. In addition to recent creations, these 500 include nearly a hundred hide, linen, and ledger paintings from around the era of the Indian wars. The 2,500 non-Western and non-Indian works include some by such celebrated artists as Copley, West, Homer, Eakins, Saint-Gaudens, and Whistler. Several important Canadian and Central American artifacts and documents are also housed in the museum.

Remarkably, these collections are largely the creation of one man, Thomas Gilcrease (1890-1962). One eighth Creek (Muskogee), the adolescent Gilcrease received a 160-acre allotment during the severalty of Indian lands. By chance, the land was rich in oil. Gilcrease's resourcefulness made him a millionaire by the age of twenty-one. At the same time, the entrepreneur was developing a passion for documents and objects related to various Indian tribes and the non-Indian settlement of the Trans-Mississippi West. His collection first opened in San Antonio in 1942 and reopened in Tulsa in 1949. During a business downturn in the early 1950s, Gilcrease worked out a plan with Tulsa that would permit him to both recapitalize and to eventually donate and endow a publicly owned museum. Today, Thomas Gilcrease's museum is owned and administered by the city of Tulsa.

For much of its first twenty-five years, the Gilcrease was a richly stocked but under-utilized local museum. Then, in 1987, a $12,000,000 renovation introduced up-to-date installation, doubled the gallery space, and created an innovative "open storage" system. This system allows visitors to see many of the 250,000 Indian artifacts not on regular exhibit. The museum has also been more visibly involved in cooperative projects with living Indian artists and tradition keepers in the past ten years. An experienced museum director, J. Brooks Joyner, arrived in 1996, and the museum has since increased its scope. The Gilcrease may now be entering an era of trend setting exhibitions and important collaborations. One evidence of this was the recent Thomas Moran exhibition, one of the most imposing U.S. art exhibits of 1998.

Among the Gilcrease works recommended by *Journal of the Indian Wars* are John Wesley Jarvis, *Black Hawk and His Son, Whirling Thunder*; Charles Bird King, *Prophet Shawanese—Brother of Tecumsi* [sic]; Frederic Remington, *Battle of War Bonnet Creek*, also *Missing* and *Wounded Bunkie* (a bronze); Charles M. Russell, *Her Heart Is on the Ground*; Charles Schreyvogel, *Breaking Through the Line* and *Custer's Demand*. When works by Charles Catlin and Alfred Jacob Miller are displayed, it may also be possible to see Catlin's *U.S. Dragoons Meeting Comanches* or Miller's *Fort Laramie or Fort William on the Laramie*.

The Gilcrease will host two especially important exhibits in 1999: "Symbols of Faith and Belief: Art of the Native American Church" (January 22-April 25) and "Down from the Shimmering Sky: Masks of the Northwest Coast" (August 20-November 7).

Visitor information—Gallery hours: 9:00 a.m. to 5:00 p.m. Tuesday through Saturday, and 11:00 a.m. to 5:00 p.m. Sundays and federal holidays. Suggested admission donation: U.S. $3.00 per individual or $5.00 per family. Location: 1400 Gilcrease Road (exit marked on US 64 West). Barrier-free access. Phone: 918-586-2700; toll free 1-888-655-2278. Web site: http://www.gilcrease.org. Facilities: Gilcrease Museum Shop, Rendezvous Restaurant. Languages: English, some materials in Spanish.

JIW staff,
with the assistance of Ken Busby, Gilcrease Museum

Gilcrease Journal recently won "best periodical" honors in the competition of the American Association of Museums (AAM). To discover why, readers may wish to order a copy of the spring 1998 issue. The articles include a profusely illustrated piece on Cheyenne ledger art at the Gilcrease (with many scenes of counting coup) and an informative section on Remington sculpture. (See this issue's book reviews for more on ledger art). Single copies are U.S. $10.00 (plus $2.00 domestic postage) from the Gilcrease Museum Shop, 1400 Museum Road, Tulsa, OK 74127-2100.

Indian Wars

Organizational, Tribal, and Museum News

Visitors to Little Bighorn Battlefield National Monument are often surprised to learn how little of the battlefield is protected within park boundaries. This is particularly true of the "Reno-Benteen" portion of the battlefield, the area where Marcus Reno's detachment held out under siege for a day past the annihilation of George A. Custer's troopers. The Custer Battlefield Protection Committee has been the most important group in acquiring additional land for protection. Recently, the committee was offered the opportunity to buy a tract of land that includes Reno's skirmish lines in the Little Bighorn valley, Reno's retreat route to the siege site on the overlooking bluffs, and the probable area of Sitting Bull's Lakota village. The tract of roughly 500 acres is being offered for sale for $1,700.000. As the land lies on an interstate highway frontage road, it is important to acquire the land before commercial development takes place.

To make a donation, or for more information, write to the Custer Battlefield Protection Committee, P. O. Box 7, Hardin, MT 59034. The committee is led by Jim Court, a superintendent at the battlefield for ten years and a professional history and natural history guide (Action Travel/Custer Tours). Jim can be reached at custertours@juno.com (406-665-1876). *Journal of the Indian Wars* (*JIW*) will carry regular updates on this important and worthwhile project.

The Battle of Fallen Timbers, Ohio (1794) ranks as one of the most decisive engagements in North American history. In it, forces of the young United States, led by "Mad" Anthony Wayne, defeated a coalition of Great Lakes–Ohio River Basin tribes. The result guaranteed white and U.S.

domination of the region known as the "Old Northwest" and the diminishment of British authority south of Canada. Despite its importance, the battle's location was misidentified for almost two centuries. In 1995, an archaeological survey of an area slated for commercial development proved that the battle had not taken place at the traditional site (marked by a commemorative park) but over a mile to the northeast. This property is not currently accessible, but the battle positions are parallel to the southbound lane of the exit from Interstate Highway 475 to U.S. Highway 24 at Maumee.

Since the discovery of the "lost" battlefield, preservation efforts have been thwarted by controversy with both potential developers and competing jurisdictions. As *JIW* went to press, the tide seemed to have turned in favor of park status, but a complex series of negotiations between Lucas County, the city of Maumee (the site location), the city of Toledo (the property owner), and even fans of the Toledo Mudhens baseball team, was underway. In the next issue, *JIW* will present the story of the battles of Fallen Timbers, old and new. In addition, Mayor Steve Pauken of Maumee will speak of his hopes of creating the first locally owned national battlefield park, and military history archaeologist J. Michael Pratt will weigh in on his exciting discoveries at Fallen Timbers and other battlefields.

The search for another famous site, that of the Sand Creek Massacre, has had a very different outcome than did the excavation at Fallen Timbers. Sand Creek in Colorado was the location of the Cheyenne village of a "peace chief," Black Kettle. An indiscriminate attack by Colorado militia in 1864 took the lives of 150 of Black Kettle's band, largely women and children. The same band would later be attacked once again at the Battle of the Washita in 1868 (see related articles in this issue).

In July 1998, a U.S. Senate bill sponsored by Northern Cheyenne member Ben Nighthorse Campbell (R), authorized the National Park Service to find the massacre site, preparatory to the creation of a park. Excavations at the traditional marked site and adjacent areas failed to turn up serious indications of either Army ammunition or Indian camp debris. (Dr. William Lees, author of this issue's article on archaeology at Washita, was involved in the search.) In the words of search leader Richard Ellis, "When we think of battle sites on American soil, this is the only major battlefield we can't find" (*New York*

Times, August 1998). Given the strong interest in the location, by the nation as a whole and the Cheyenne and Arapaho tribes in particular, it is possible that further efforts will be made to find the site of the Sand Creek Massacre.

The American Battlefield Protection Program (ABBP) has, since 1990, enormously benefited military history researchers and preservationists. Its recent accomplishments include:

a) completion of a series of one-page synopses on every American Civil War battle site of significance (including Indian wars battles occurring 1861-1865);

b) the beginnings of a similar project on battle sites of the American Revolutionary War and the War of 1812 (including related Indian conflicts);

c) grants to groups seeking to document and interpret the battlefields at Fort Recovery (1791) and Fallen Timbers (1794) in Ohio and of George Crook's 1876 campaigns against the Cheyenne and "Sioux" Indians.

The ABPP is also responsible for holding annual conferences on battlefield preservation. For more information on the program and its on-line and printed publications, see its web site at http://www2.cr.nps.gov/abpp/batpubs.htm or request its printed newsletter from Editor, *Battlefield Update*, National Park Service, American Battlefield Protection Program, 1849 C Street, NW (NC330), Washington, DC 20240.

The *Order of the Indian Wars* held its eighteenth national assembly at Jackson Hole, Wyoming, in September 1998. Its focus was on "Battles of the Fur Trade," with an outstanding series of lectures and tours by Dr. Fred Gowans of Brigham Young University. Participants from as distant as Australia toured the site of the Battle of Pierre's Hole, the locations of six of the famous fur trade "rendezvous," and Yellowstone National Park. Next year's assembly is tentatively scheduled for Amarillo, Texas, where participants will tour the Red River War (1874-1875) battlefields of Adobe Walls and Palo Duro Canyon, with an optional trip to the Washita Battlefield (1868) in Oklahoma.

Journal of the Indian Wars was launched with the inspiration and cooperation of this worthwhile study, tour, and preservation group. For more information on the organization, contact Jerry L. Russell, Order of the Indian Wars, P.O. Box 7491, Little Rock, AR 72217. Membership: U.S. $20.00.

Other important conferences relevant to the Indian Wars were also held in the U.S. in 1998. The Council on America's Military Past (CAMP) held the 32nd Annual Military History Conference in Lexington, Kentucky, in May. Though many sites toured by CAMP were American Civil War sites, the organization also visited the reconstructions of forts Harrod and Boonesborough, and the Blue Licks Battlefield, places involved in the Indian wars of the American Revolutionary War. CAMP's *Headquarters Heliogram* quarterly is a comprehensive news source on military historical sites in the U.S. CAMP may also have a web site in operation by the publication of this issue. [Council on America's Military Past, P.O. Box 1151, Fort Meyer, VA 22211. Subscriptions: U.S. $35; contributing memberships: $50.]

The Little Bighorn Associates, which frequently concentrates on George A. Custer and the Sioux War of 1876-1877, held its annual meeting in Charlottesville, Virginia, in July. [Conventions: Mike McCormack, Bismarck State College, 1500 Edwards Ave., Bismarck, ND 58501; membership: Bill Serritella, Treasurer LBHA, P.O. Box 1160, LaGrange Park, IL 60526-1160. North American membership: $30.00, overseas: U.S. $40.00.]

The new Washita Battlefield National Historic Site celebrated a symposium, "Washita Battlefield: Past, Present, and Future," in Cheyenne, Oklahoma, in November 1998.

One of the most active and productive regional Indian wars study and preservation groups is the Fort Phil Kearny/Bozeman Trail Association. During 1998, the association continued the acquisition of the Sullivant Hills, protecting the view of the horizon from Fort Phil Kearny Historic Site. The hills were a major landmark in the constant fighting around the fort during the Bozeman Trail or Red Cloud's War (1866-1867). The group is continuing to seek private and corporate donors for land payments. [Fort Phil

Kearny/Bozeman Trail Association, P.O. Box 5013, Sheridan, WY 82801. Membership U.S. $15.]

*T*he Logan's Fort Foundation was formed to save the site of Logan's Fort/St. Asaph, Kentucky, from the likelihood of real estate development. The fort was one of the most important pioneer fortifications on the Trans-Appalachian frontier of North America and was located at the junction of several important routes west. The location was not pinpointed archaeologically until 1996 (when the skeleton of a defender killed during an Indian siege in 1777 was located). The organization needs to acquire $25,000 in donations to qualify for a government matching grant of $100,000. [Logan's Fort Foundation, P.O. Box 1775, Stanford, KY 40484. Membership U.S. $10.]

*O*ne of the least known—and most tragic—of North American Indian conflicts was the Texas-Cherokee war. This conflict was due largely to the efforts of Republic of Texas President Mirabeau B. Lamar (1838-1840) to force relocated Cherokees and the remnants of local tribes to vacate their lands. The war ended with a running battle in which Cherokee chief Bowles was killed. A new organization, the American Indian Cultural Society, is acquiring seventy acres of the Neches battlefield, where Bowles was killed. The land is located in the community of Redland, twelve miles west of Tyler, Texas. Today, there is a Texas marker on the site, but the stone is not accessible by automobile. The group is seeking funds to complete the land purchase, refurbish a building for use as a visitor contact point, and eventually build a pan-Indian cultural center. The site will also serve as a shrine for the Cherokee dead. [Information: Lynn Vitasek, P.O. Box 177847, Irving, TX 75017-7847; donations: Eagle Douglas, Box 1884, DeSoto, TX 75123.]

*F*ort Phantom Hill, Texas, was briefly (1851-1854), a important post in a line of forts parallel to the Great Comanche War Trail. The site is unusual in that it has been interpreted and made accessible by a private ranch owner, Jim Alexander. In mid-1998, a group of faculty and students from Texas Tech University carried out a five week excavation of the location and found it to be in "pristine" condition archaeologically. A Fort Phantom Hill Foundation has now been been formed to increase public awareness of the site.

Another Texas fort in the same chain, Fort McKavett, is best known for its role in the Red River War (1874-1875). The post, located in Fort McKavett State Historical Park, is considered one of the "top three preserved frontier forts in Texas." Continued restoration work has now raised the number of roofed buildings at the park to sixteen.

The Mashantucket Pequot tribe has enjoyed a remarkable history. Its members managed to survive the genocidal Pequot Wars of 1636-1638, centuries of neglect and poverty on a small reservation, and repeated battles for land rights in U.S. Federal courts. Since the 1980s, the tribe has become known for its significant legal victories and its pioneering role in Indian gambling and resort operations. Since August of 1998, the Pequot have had another cause for celebrity: the Mashantucket Pequot Museum and Research Center. This new facility, a $135,000,000 investment, tells the story of the Pequot Nation, as well as of other tribes, and of the natural history and cultural evolution of the region.

By all accounts, the museum contains one of the most impressive arrays of state-of-the-art museum exhibits and audiovisual productions of any in the U.S. These include environmental simulations, dioramas and models, computer interactions, and thirteen film and video productions. Two features, a reconstruction of a Pequot fort and village found on the site and the film "The Witness" (a half hour production on the 1637 massacre at the Pequot fort in Mystic), have a particular bearing on Indian wars. The museum, located seven miles from Mystic, Connecticut, in the community of Mashantucket, promises to be among the highlights of a visit to New England by anyone interested in American Indian history.

The Ah-Tha-Thi-Ki Museum in Florida is another up-to-date tribal museum. This new (1997) facility uses computers, dioramas, nature trails, and a "living village" to tell the story of the Seminole Tribe. Although the Seminole wars are not neglected, the museum's strengths appear to be its exhibits on spiritual beliefs and traditional folk ways. The museum is located seventeen miles north of Interstate Highway 75 ("Alligator Alley"), between Naples and Fort Lauderdale.

JIW also maintains a news page, with updates, excerpts, and interviews, on the world wide web. The internet address for Savas Publishing Company is http://www.savaspublishing.com. Savas Publishing offers a full line of original Civil War and military and general history books. Visit us when you have a moment. Your comments are encouraged and appreciated.

*   *   *

*O*rganizations, tribes, and museums are invited to submit relevant news for publication in *JIW*. Our mailing address is: Michael A. Hughes, Editor, *Journal of the Indian Wars*, 834 East Sixth Street, Box E, Ada, OK 74820. News submissions should include a brief, abstracted version of any information and are subject to editing. The submission of news automatically includes the right for *JIW* to publish the information and/or post the information on our web site.

Book Reviews

Warrior Artists: Historic Cheyenne and Kiowa Indian Ledger Art Drawn by Making Medicine and Zotom, by Herman J. Viola, with Joseph D. and George P. Horse Capture (Washington: National Geographic Society, 1998), 125pp. Color prints and photographs, bibliography. Cloth, $35.00.

For centuries, warriors of the North American Plains recorded battles and acts of bravery on buffalo and other animal skins. "Ledger art" or "ledgerbook art," a general term for Indian art on paper, developed in the 1800s as the tribes acquired notebooks, army and store ledgers, and single pages through trade and raiding. At first, the artists working on paper continued an ancient pictographic approach—descriptive yet very stylized. By mid-century, however, they had creatively adapted both to new media, which now included colored pencils, and to exposure to European styles. For example, while figures had originally been shown in profile, they began to appear in three-quarter and even full frontal views as well.

As an art genre that is now both critically acclaimed and recognized as an important ethno-historical source, ledger art has become a hot subject among scholars and publishers in the last several years. Little wonder, as most of us cannot help but be enthralled with such pieces of art and story all in one. This recent popularity may account for the production of *Warrior Artists*, despite the previous publication of part of the drawings and the difficulties involved in publishing art from a private collection.

Warrior Artists is in several ways appreciated by this reviewer. National Geographic books are welcomed like family, and *Warrior Artists* will be no exception. Color reproductions of any ledger art are very much appreciated, and here is a whole book of them meeting National Geographic's high standards. Each drawing is faithfully reproduced as to content and color. Opposite each drawing is a commentary by Joseph and/or George Horse Capture.

Herman Viola's introductory remarks provide an adequate background for understanding the artists and their art. As Viola explains, the drawings' creators were among seventy-two militant Plains warriors and chiefs shipped east to be imprisoned in Fort Marion, Florida (today Castillo de San Marcos National

Monument) in 1875. During their three years there, the prisoners produced a large body of art portraying their life before and after captivity. *Warrior Artists* comes from a sketchbook of Making Medicine (Okuhhatuh), a Cheyenne, and Zotom, a Kiowa, two of the most gifted prisoners.

Unfortunately, and this is one of the major drawbacks of this book, Viola did not cite his sources. He lists in the bibliography seven books and a set of government records, acknowledging that most of his information came from these records and from the published memoirs of Capt. Henry Pratt. Except in the cases where Viola quotes Pratt, we are provided with no citations of sources. Consequently, the text loses some authority, and the volume's use is largely limited to art appreciation. Fortunately, the artwork is the book's strength and main attraction in any case.

Another problem is poor editing. For example, on page four is a photograph of the Cheyenne captives as they arrive at the fort. The caption on the adjacent page begins "Capt. Richard Henry Pratt and prisoners. . . ." Captain Pratt is not in the photograph. The drawing on page forty-eight clearly shows four men on horseback. Yet the commentary refers to "four of the five hunters." Lastly, the drawing on page sixty-five portrays two groups of Indians, one walking and one mounted, approaching Fort Sill, Oklahoma. The commentary for the picture states, "While a small group of Indians watch, an officer drills his cavalry troop." However, there are no troops visible, only a single mounted soldier watching the Indians.

Another shortcoming is that the commentaries by Joseph and George Horse Capture are very limited. My sense is that they were placed under severe space restrictions. There is much to be learned about Indian culture in each drawing, but the points most readers will miss, such as the meanings of the colors, symbols, and accoutrements, are often not discussed. There are some descriptions but too few for a thorough understanding of the details. In short, the text fails to "tell the story," a major disappointment to this reviewer. The Horse Captures are known internationally for their expertise, and more words from them would have been appreciated. What commentary they do provide is crisp, direct, and (except for the editing problems) accurate.

Warrior Artists is an important book in spite of the weaknesses cited above. Many of the pictures in the book, particularly those by Making Medicine, have never been published, so this is a major addition to the body of Fort Marion Indian art revealed to the public. This book makes it possible to trace the progression of each artist's skills and techniques and to confirm which earlier or similar works were done by the two men. For those of us unable to get to the art and other resources in the National Archives or the Smithsonian or the Denver Public Library, a book such as this is indispensable for the study of Indian art. It is welcome evidence of a growing public awareness of this art style and will hopefully encourage others with ledger art in private collections to share it with the public.

Rodney G. Thomas, Colonel, U.S. Army, Retired

Cheyenne Dog Soldiers: A Ledgerbook History of Coups and Combat, by Jean Afton, David Fridtjof Halaas, and Andrew E. Masich, with Richard N. Ellis (Niwot: Colorado Historical Society and the University Press of Colorado, 1997), 400pp. Color prints and photographs, maps, appendices, notes, bibliography, index. Cloth, $49.95.

On those amazing occasions when a college press book sells out before all reviews are in, one of three things must have been true: the author had many kind friends, the press acted too cautiously, or word spread quickly that it was an extraordinary book. Whether or not the first two possibilities about *Cheyenne Dog Soldiers* are true, the third is certainly accurrate. This is the kind of work that should serve as a model for similar research and publishing efforts.

The history of the ledgerbook featured in *Cheyenne Dog Soldiers* is as remarkable as its contents. In the 1860s, the encroachments of Colorado-bound miners and the removal of troops to fight in the American Civil War spurred raids and reprisals by the tribes of the Central Plains. Evidence suggests the unused book was among the plunder of a raid along the South Platte River in 1865. For several years, the ledgerbook was the possession of the Dog Men or Dog Soldiers, perhaps the most aggressive and feared of the Cheyenne military societies. At least thirty identifiable Dog Soldier artists recorded acts of valor on these pages. Some scenes depict the taking of lives or captives. Many are of the most honored deed, counting coup (touching an enemy).

On July 11, 1869, the Fifth U.S. Cavalry Regiment and three companies of Pawnee scouts swept through the camp of the Dog Solders. The ledgerbook was among the items captured. In 1903, the record was left to the Colorado

Historical Society. It remained largely unknown until the collaborators on *Cheyenne Dog Soldiers*—historians, anthropologists, and Cheyenne tradition-keepers—produced this volume. Scholars of Western history in general, and the Indian wars in particular, owe a debt of thanks to the Colorado Colorado Historical Society and the Colorado University Press.

In the introduction and prologue, the authors describe the bitter and turbulent history of the Cheyenne in the 1860s, the evolution of the ledgerbook style, and the means of identifying individual artists. This is followed with a detailed commentary on each drawing. The discussion of artistic styles is markedly better than that in a similar recent study, *Warrior Artists* (Washington: National Geographic Society, 1998). However, while the prints in *Cheyenne Dog Soldiers* are of good quality, they are smaller and less brilliant than those portrayed in *Warrior Artists*.

The customs and protocol of the warfare in each drawing of *Cheyenne Dog Soldiers* are fully described. Likewise, the Indian and white costumes and accoutrements are fully discussed. This is often aided by the use of photographs. Because of the purely military focus of the Dog Soldiers, readers will not get as much information on general Cheyenne culture as they might from the briefer commentaries in *Warrior Artists*. They will, however, obtain a much better understanding of the drawings themselves in *Dog Soldiers*, which includes maps, a comprehensive chronology of the events from 1864-69, notes on individual artists, a glossary of terms ranging from "abalone shell terminal" to "worsted lace," and even an appendix on ledgerbook structure.

The authors' research in *Dog Soldiers* is so thorough that the exact time and place of many of the events in the ledgerbook are established using written sources. Conversely, the Cheyenne drawings are shown to be valuable historical records in their own right. In addition, a number of drawings can be readily appreciated for their artistic merit (for example, White Bird's depiction of soldiers "all in a row" [Plate 22] or Bear Man's picture of "a running fight" [Plate 81]). Ultimately, perhaps the greatest value of *Cheyenne Dog Soldiers* is that it offers us our best opportunity to enter the minds of the long-departed warrior-artists who created the scenes.

Michael A. Hughes, Ada, OK

Scalp Dance: Indian Warfare on the High Plains, 1865-1879, by Thomas Goodrich. (Mechanicsburg: Stackpole Books, 1997), 352pp. Illustrations, maps, biblio., index, d.j. Cloth, $32.95.

Scalp Dance is a "blast from the past," a book that dares to suggest that whites as well as Indians were victims in the Indian wars. This reviewer is both surprised and delighted to find that this book was chosen as a selection of Doubleday's Military Book Club. Perhaps its selection heralds what this reviewer regards as the long overdue demise of the current preference for sensitivity over objectivity. This reviewer's opinion having been clearly stated, let's look at *Scalp Dance.*

Scalp Dance is highly reminiscent of such older books as Fairfax Downey's *Indian Fighting Army* or Paul Wellman's *Death on the Prairie.* Like them, it is a synopsis of events in a thirty-four year period of Indian warfare on the North American Plains. However, the author chose the year 1879, rather than the usual 1890, to end his book. Perhaps Goodrich felt that enough has been written about the late events at Wounded Knee, South Dakota, of 1890. Also, neither Downey nor Wellman uses the participants' own accounts to nearly the degree used by Goodrich. It is the excerpting of firsthand accounts that strengthens *Scalp Dance.* Goodrich allows much of the story to be told by those who lived it, and it is their conclusions about the Indian wars that he presents.

When Goodrich offers his own evaluations, he sometimes gets into trouble. This reviewer doubts some of the author's conclusions. For example, in speaking of the Battle of Beecher Island, Colorado (1868), Goodrich states that "in the epic nine-day stand of the Arickaree [River], the major [George Forsyth] and his men had suffered a stunning defeat." I would say that it was the Cheyenne Indian force which suffered defeat. In several days' fighting, 600 warriors were unable to overwhelm fifty scouts in a nearly indefensible position on a spit of land in an almost dry riverbed. In another instance, this one in his chapter on the battle of the Rosebud (1876), Goodrich states that "[w]hat [George] Crook saw made his blood run cold—perhaps 2,500 Sioux and Northern Cheyenne warriors. . . ." If the author were using a direct quote, including this high estimate would be excusable. I'm sure that many of the soldiers in the battle felt that there were that many warriors. However, a far more accurate estimate would be only 700 to 1,000 warriors.

The bibliography for *Scalp Dance* is reasonably extensive for a Plains wars survey of this kind, but it is also remarkable for its complete absence of Indian accounts. The work is clearly a view of the Indian wars as seen exclusively by the white man. As long as one understands that, the book is a "good read." I suspect, however, that some readers of this journal may find it a bit general.

Mike Koury, Publisher, Old Army Press

The Contested Plains: Indians, Gold seekers, and the Rush to Colorado, by Elliott West (Lawrence: University Press of Colorado, 1998), 424pp. Illustrations, notes, biblio., index, d.j. Cloth, $34.95.

In *The Contested Plains*, Elliott West take a new look at the 1858 Colorado gold strike and its consequences. West focuses his study not so much on the miners and their efforts to find gold in the Rocky Mountains, but rather on the economic, environmental, and cultural impact the Gold Rush had on the Great Plains and the people who lived there. He sees the Plains as unchangeable since the beginning of time, though each new group of human dwellers attempted to mold and control the resources and wildlife according to its own needs. The Cheyenne Indians and white miners were just two such groups whose paths crossed on this "converging frontier." West particularly examines how the Cheyenne and the whites clashed over control of the Plains and over how the land would be used in the future.

Using an approach similar to that used in one of his earlier books, *The Way to the West*, the author discusses the importance of environment, among other things, on the course of human history. For example, the arrival of the horse changed the way of life of the Cheyenne, causing them to migrate to the Plains and to challenge other tribes for control of prime hunting and grazing land. In so doing, the Cheyenne created a vision of the frontier that suited their needs. This vision was disrupted by the encroachment of gold-seeking whites and their view of the uses of the Plains and of what life on the Plains should encompass. The whites needed buildings, towns, businesses, and roads. More importantly, they wanted the neutralization of the Indian nations already living there. As West notes, "the [G]old [R]ush transformed mid-America and undercut the life of nomadic Native Americans." In the end, the Cheyenne were economically, culturally, and environmentally overwhelmed by the consequences of the white vision for the land.

Well researched, *Contested Plains* covers a diverse variety of topics and ideas. West works his way from the circumstances of the earliest Plains dwellers, through conditions on the roads leading to the gold strikes, to the traditional ways of life of the Plains Indians as these collapse. *Contested Plains* imparts little new information about the Gold Rush era, but the author relates the information in a fresh and thought-provoking way. West's approach is reminiscent of that used in *Changes in the Land* by William Cronon or the works of Francis Jennings.

Contested Plains is a good study but is marred by many grammatical and editing problems, including several badly jumbled sentences. Even so, West should be commended for his latest effort.

Paul Beck, *Wesleyan Lutheran College*

Hollow Victory: The White River Expedition of 1879 and the Battle of Milk Creek, by Mark E. Miller (Niwot: University Press of Colorado, 1997), 249pp. Illustrations, maps, appendices, notes, biblio., index, d.j. Cloth, $27.50.

On September 29, 1879, a U.S. Army column numbering some 180 men was attacked by a force of Ute Indians while en route from Fort Fred Steele, Wyoming, to the White River Ute Indian Agency near present Meeker, Colorado. The troops, under the command of Maj. Thomas T. Thornburgh, were traveling to the fort in response to repeated requests from the Ute Agent, Nathan Meeker, for military assistance to control what he regarded as his unruly charges at the agency.

Angry at the presence of the soldiers on their reservation, the Utes ambushed Thornburgh's command near Milk Creek, some twenty-miles from the agency. Thornburgh himself was killed early on, and his command was besieged for nearly six days until finally rescued by a relief column under the command of Col. Wesley Merritt.

While Thornburgh's command was fighting for its life, Meeker and nine of his employees were slain by enraged Utes who also took two women and three children hostage, including Mrs. Meeker and her daughter. The hostages were later released unharmed. The agency massacre, coupled with Thornburgh's defeat, very nearly brought on a war with the Utes. Fortunately, that development was averted through the determined efforts of the Ute chief, Ouray, as well as Special Agent Charles Francis Adams and others.

The Battle of Milk River, Colorado, is a striking illustration of how overreaction in a tense situation can lead to tragic consequences. As the author reminds us, it also stands as yet another monument to the perils of misunderstanding and miscommunication.

In recreating the Battle of Milk River, Mark Miller has done an outstanding job of sifting through much contradictory evidence to provide us with a clear, well written account of one of the "longest sustained" fights in the history of the Western Indian wars.

Hollow Victory is likely to become the standard treatment of this unfortunate affair for some time to come.

Jerry Keenan, Boulder, CO

The Chiricahua Apache Prisoners of War, Fort Sill, 1894-1914, by John Anthony Turcheneske, Jr. (Niwot: University Press of Colorado, 1997), 232pp., photographs, notes, biblio., index, d.j. Cloth, $29.95.

The use of words such as "callously," "cynically," "egregious," "reprehensible," "ignominies," "tragedy," "unconscionable," and "injustice" seems to suggest that this is not a neutral work—and these are all in the preface, less than two pages in length! Turcheneske's book is not neutral, but it is excellent.

Author Turcheneske believes that the story he tells in this book is "little-known." As an Oklahoma historian, this reviewer would take issue with the author's belief that the story is obscure. The author may be on more solid ground when he suggests that the story he narrates "occupies a unique niche in Native American history" (xi).

The focal point of the work is the twenty-seven year period of captivity endured by the Chiracahua Apaches (Diné) following the surrender of Geronimo's (Goyakla's) band. Nearly 400 of the Chiracahua were uprooted and exiled from their home around San Carlos, Arizona. For most of the next three decades, they were kept at Fort Sill, Oklahoma. Indeed, the Fort Sill area was promised to the Chiricahuas as their permanent reservation. They were even given a herd of some 1,000 cattle to build an economic base. That herd grew to about 10,000 under their tutelage. But in 1903, the military reneged on its promise and decided to turn Fort Sill into a field artillery training installation. In 1913, those Apaches who wished to do so were moved to New Mexico. Those remaining in Oklahoma had their cattle sold off and were given a mere 160-acre allotment beyond the post on former Kiowa and Comanche lands.

Turcheneske's chapter titles reveal his opinion of the Apaches' situation: "An Innocent People Are Taken Captive," or "Foreclosure of Chiricahua Rights to Fort Sill: Establishment of the U.S. Army Field School of Fire," and "Liberated into Penury: A Most Parsimonious Chiricahua Allotment in Oklahoma."

His epilogue is meaningfully entitled "Quest for Freedom: A Case of Justice Denied." In this epilogue, the author insists powerfully that the story he has told is "unparalleled in the annals of American Indian-Federal government relations" (181). The only possible exception, he suggests, is the nearly total extermination of the Pequots as a consequence of the war waged against them by the English settlers of Massachusetts in the 1630s. With equal force, Turcheneske asserts that "[i]t is an incontrovertible fact that the War Department was morally and legally obligated to transfer ownership of Fort Sill to the Chiricahua Apache prisoners of war for their reservation" (p. 184), and that "[t]he great irony of the whole heart-wrenching Chiricahua sagas is that the white participants therein were also prisoners; that is to say, they were chained to and victimized by their own and others' attitudes, prejudices, and preconceived ideas about how policies relating to Indian warfare might best be implemented" (186).

The author is on considerably weaker ground when he falls into the trap of comparing victimizations—comparing the Chiricahuas' fate with that of Confederate, German, and Japanese victims of war (182)—and when he ends the books with a bit of counter-factual history: "Had justice been rendered throughout their quest for freedom, the economic, social, cultural, and political disaster that befell the Chiricahuas after their release from military custody would not have transpired" (187). We cannot really know this, can we?

Turcheneske's work is thoroughly documented and contains an impressive bibliography. However, this reviewer could not understand the distinction made between the "Bibliography" and the book's "Additional Sources." The work is also nicely illustrated with both photographs and maps. The University Press of Colorado is to be congratulated for producing such an attractive volume.

Any reader of *Journal of the Indian Wars* interested only in the details of military operations will be disappointed with *The Chiricahua Apache Prisoners of War*. But if that reader is willing to be reminded of still another ugly specific result of those operations, this is a good book to read.

Davis D. Joyce, East Central University (Oklahoma)

Six Weeks in the Sioux Tepees: A Narrative of Indian Captivity, by Sarah F. Wakefield, edited by June Namias (Norman: University of Oklahoma Press, 1997), illustrations, map, introduction, chronology, notes, biblio., index, d.j. Cloth, $27.95.

Lost Bird of Wounded Knee: Spirit of the Lakota, by Renée Sansom Flood (New York: Da Capo Press, 1995; paperback reprint, 1998), 384pp. Photos, notes, biblio., index. Paper, $15.95.

With My Own Eyes: A Lakota Woman Tells Her People's History, by Susan Bordeaux Bettelyoun and Josephine Waggoner, edited by Emily Levine (Lincoln: University of Nebraska Press, 1998) 187pp. Photos, maps, chronology, notes, index, d.j. Cloth, $35.00.

As historian Neil Mangum observes in the dedication to the issue, far too little has been written about the involvement of women in the Indian wars. The unique situations of three such women are the subject of three interesting recent books. Each of the three participants experienced the cultural and military conflict between whites and Indians. For the first the result was enlightenment; for the second, tragedy; and for the third, ambiguity.

In some ways, *Six Weeks in the Sioux Tepees* carries on a long tradition of female "captivity narratives" dating back to the 1600s. Sarah F. Wakefield, however, was more fortunate, more articulate, and more empathetic than previous authors. Her narrative consequently ranges from fascinating anecdotes to moving demands for social justice.

In 1862, the wartime absence of a Federal authority that seldom kept its promises, the callousness of Indian agents and merchants, and the incitement of young warriors provoked a series of attacks by the Eastern Dakota Indians of Minnnesota that took the lives of 500 whites. In addition, many hostages were taken, including Mrs. Wakefield, a young doctor's wife. Although the author experienced physical hardship in captivity, she also experienced many acts of consideration, particularly from Chaska, a man she came to regard as her savior. Believing that the Indians had themselves been victims before becoming aggressors, Wakefield wrote with unusual sympathy of the Dakota prisoners of war at the end of the conflict. The book seems written, in part, as a plea for divine justice after Chaska's execution as the result of a clerical error.

Editor June Namias helpfully provides readers with background material on the evolution of the war and the life of Sarah Wakefield. The editor particularly tries to conclude why Wakefield, unique among the white women of Minnesota, stepped forward to defend the Dakota. Though not the book's goal, the wealth of detail in the author's narrative and the editor's introduction and notes make *Six Weeks* a worthwhile source on the "Minnesota Uprising" as well as an "good read."

Readers may remember hearing of the remains of a Lakota woman known as Lost Bird (Zintkala Nuni) being brought from California to South Dakota for a celebrated reburial in 1991. In *Lost Bird of Wounded Knee*, author Renée Sansom Flood has provided a well researched and beautifully written account of Lost Bird's sad life.

Lost Bird was a infant survivor of the Wounded Knee Massacre (1890). Her mother was among the 150 Lakota, largely women and children, found dead after that explosive incident involving Indian apocalyptics and white cavalrymen. Several weeks later, the child was adopted as a "relic of the Indian wars" by an unsavory and opportunistic officer and attorney named Leonard Colby. The child's adopted mother, Clara Colby, was a suffragette whose life would prove as melodramatic as Lost Bird's would prove tragic; By adolescence, Lost Bird found herself rootless, abused or exploited by whites and unsuccessful in her attempts to be accepted by Indians. When she expired of cardiac failure around the age of thirty, she died both literally and figuratively of a broken heart. Since then, Lost Bird has posthumously been appropriated as a symbol of the failure of Indian assimilation into white culture.

While *Lost Bird* offers readers very limited information on the Indian wars, reading this book will seem a natural extension of interest in those conflicts. Renée Sansom Flood often seems eager to leap to conjecture in expressing her character's thoughts and words. However, the author deserves credit for producing a text that is unusually colorful and gripping. Da Capo Press is to be commended for producing a very affordable paperback version of a recent hardback book.

While assimilation ended in tragedy for Lost Bird, it seems to have provided no more than unselfconscious ambiguity for Susan Bordeaux Bettelyoun and her collaborator Josephine Waggoner. As explained in *With My Own Eyes*, Bettelyoun was the child of a Lakota Sioux mother and a French-American father. The value system she expresses (the manuscript was written in the 1930s) is often that of the white world. At the same time, Bettelyoun and Waggoner wrote out of a conviction that white histories carried many misconceptions about their Lakota relatives. Further, the narrative frequently involves a sense of chronology and priority that the editor identifies as uniquely Indian.

Students of the Plains wars know that any book that begins "I was born at Fort Laramie . . ." and shortly continues with ". . . I saw my father bury Lieutenant Grattan" will obviously be of interest to them. With *My Own Eyes* contains a good deal of information on Indian warfare on the Central Plains, as well as details about the reservation system and Indian education. The difficulty is that family and documentary history are so thoroughly blended that it is difficult to tell when the text can be regarded as a primary source. Still, readers and researchers will find a wealth of intriguing historical, cultural, and biographical details in the book; the editor's extensive notes are a real benefit and will assist the reader in developing further interests.

With My Own Eyes is rare in that it would be equally useful in classes as diverse as those on westward expansion, American studies, women's studies, and ethnic studies. And, like the other two books reviewed above, this one can be read and enjoyed by specialists and nonspecialists alike.

Rev. Bruce Welsh, Cheyenne, WY

Swamp Sailors in the Seminole War, by George E. Buker (Gainesville: University Press of Florida, 1975; reprint 1997.) Illustrations, maps, notes, biblio., index, 148pp. Paper, $16.95.

Swamp Sailors in the Second Seminole War is based on the 1969 Ph.D. Dissertation entitled "Riverine Warfare: Naval Combat in the Second Seminole War, 1835-1842," by George E. Buker, now a professor of history at Jacksonville [Florida] University. It was fortunate for military history enthusiasts that he made the information in his dissertation more widely available by writing *Swamp Sailors*, and the University Press of Florida is to be commended for reprinting it.

Those seeking a general discussion of the Second Seminole War will be disappointed by the book, as Buker concentrates primarily on the U.S. Navy's participation in this most unusual conflict. However, this focus is what makes the book both original and significant. *Swamp Sailors* is the first examination of the Navy's participation in the Second Seminole War, the largest part it ever played in an Indian war. (Besides the prominent Army and Navy presence in Florida, nearly the entire U.S. Marine corps fought there, including its commandant, Archibald Henderson.)

In rereading the book, this reviewer was again struck by the obvious parallels between the nineteenth century fighting in Florida and that over a century later in Vietnam. This seems especially true when Buker so expertly describes the riverine warfare in the Everglades. Anyone familiar with the "brown water" missions of the modern U.S. Navy in the Mekong Delta and similar shallow water environments in Vietnam will enjoy learning about Lts. Levi Powell and John McLaughlin. McLaughlin's novel "Mosquito Fleet" was composed of canoes and flat-bottom boats which, manned by joint combat teams of army and navy personnel, operated on the inland waters of the coastal region as well as in the vast swamp lands; Lieutenant Powell's—and especially McLaughlin's—operations anticipated the development of similar riverine warfare in Southeast Asia from 1962 to 1975. [Note: The reviewer was a U.S. Navy flight surgeon from 1972-1975.]

Buker's portrayal of the dank Everglades confronting the Navy forces is vivid and will likely trigger sharp memories for any who have served in similar conditions. At one point he writes, "The vegetation was so dense in most places that the sun's rays seldom penetrated to the earth's surface. Water stood year-round with little movement, and a thick layer of green slime covered most of the area. When this surface was disturbed, foul toxic vapors arose which caused the men to retch" (104).

The only substantive criticism that can be made of the book is Buker's occasional use of terms like "brave," "squaw," and "red men" to describe the Seminoles. Any future edition of *Swamp Sailors* should omit such outdated words.

In sum, this book will be of interest to veterans (especially Vietnam veterans), students of military history, and Indian War enthusiasts. Although probably a bit narrow in subject for general readers, it belongs in every library in Florida.

Thomas P. Senter, M.D.

Along the Texas Fort Trail, by B. W. Aston and Jonathan Taylor (Denton: University of North Texas Press, 1997, paper revised edition). 165pp. Biblio., maps and illustrations. $10.95.

This book is one of the better guides to the Texas Highway Department's Texas Forts Trail. It provides a much needed source of information for anyone interested in following the blue and white signs along the designated roads and highways of the forts tour route. The book will wear well since it has two good maps on the bound pages, rather than on flimsy, fold-out pages. The size of this paperback is convenient, and the format is easy to understand.

However, this book could use an overhaul. For example, the authors simply mention that Fort Griffin was a center for Ranald Mackenzie's campaigns in 1871, 1872, and 1874 (33), without adding that the fort was the main supply base for his column in the important 1874 Red River War. And there are several errors in the text. Page 75 states that "Mackenzie reached Fort Concho on February 25, 1871, as Colonel of the Fourth Cavalry." However, military post returns show that Mackenzie was still in command of the Forty-First Infantry —a black or "Buffalo Soldier" regiment—at that time. The colonel did not receive command of the Fourth Cavalry until December of 1871. Similarly, the authors claim (91) that Mackenzie arrived at Fort McKavett on March 15, 1869 (actually March 16) to take command of the Twenty-Fourth infantry. In fact, the

Twenty-Fourth Infantry—another black regiment—did not even exist until October of 1869, when it was formed through a consolidation of two older units. The section on Texas Highway 190 also contains an error (92-93), when it alleges that the 1936 public works project reconstruction of the ruins of the Spanish post near Menard are those of Presidio San Luis de Las Amarillas (which was founded in 1757, not 1751 as this book states). Actually, the ruins represent the 1761-70 Presidio de San Sabà, a stone fortification, and not the earlier Presidio San Luis, which was of wood.

A good overall editing and some revision before the book's next printing should make *Along the Texas Forts Trail* an even better guidebook than it is in its current state.

Edwin F. Quiroz, Fort McKavett State Historic Park, Texas

Video Reviews

A History of Native Americans (Indians of North American Video Collection I, 1993); *Apache* (Indians of North America Video Collection II, 1994). Schlessinger Video Productions (Library Video Company, P.O. Box 580, Wynnewood, PA 19096; 800-843-3629). VHS format; thirty minutes each. $39.95 each title or $399.50 per ten title collection.

Apache and *A History of Native Americans* belong to two different sets of videos produced by Schlessinger Media, a company which specializes in the production of multicultural and health/environment educational materials. Though designed for use with U.S. school grades four through ten, the two videos reviewed never talk down to their intended audience. Both, as a result, can be appreciated by most adults. Production values in *Apache* and *History* are high, with some beautiful videography, and the two titles have won "Telly" awards.

The two videos, especially *Apache*, are at their best when creating an impression of Indian culture and when using interviews with contemporary Indians that speak of their connection to their tribes' pasts.

There are no overt factual errors in the programs. Several common misconceptions about Indians are refuted (such as the assumption that Geronimo was a war leader rather than a shaman), and an effort is made to at least mention some of the subtler explanations for conflicts.

The videos' most common weakness is overgeneralization, most obviously and predictably in the thirty minute *History*. For example, the videos can easily leave the impression that all groups of North American Indians were primarily buffalo hunters. Whites are often portrayed as one dimensionally as Indians were until recent years. Also, like too many other documentary films, these use historic prints and photographs of vastly different peoples and periods as if they were completely interchangeable.

Other "warrior" tribes covered in the two series are the Cheyenne, the Comanche, the Iroquois, the Seminole (among the ten titles of collection I), and the Creek and Crow (among the ten titles of collection II).

Neither of the two videos is "indispensable" for adult students of the Indian wars (although *Apache* could serve as an enlightening and interesting window upon that tribe's rich culture). Still, the two videos reviewed are superior to a good many of the so-called "multicultural" classroom resources currently being thrown together to meet current demand. These can certainly be recommended for inclusion in school and public libraries.

Michael A. Hughes, Ada, OK

Brief Reviews and Book Notes

Voice of the Old Wolf: Lucullus Virgil McWhorter and the Nez Perce Indians, by Steven Ross Evans (Pullman: Washington State University Press, 1996). 198pp. Illustrations, notes, biblio. Paper, $19.95.

The story of the Nez Perce (Numiipu) Indians' courageous and unsuccessful flight towards freedom in Canada (1877) has often been told. Less well known is the story of their return to Washington state from a heartbreaking confinement in the Oklahoma Indian Territory and the erosion of their culture that followed. During this critical stage, a rancher named Lucullus Virgil

McWhorter befriended the Nez Perce. For the rest of his life, McWhorter would do all he could to aid the tribe in its court battles, to encourage the preservation of its traditions, and to preserve the accounts of the non-reservation or "patriot" leaders. The famous Nez Perce War history *Hear Me, My Chiefs!* (1925) was only one of the accomplishments of a man whom the old warriors regarded as their brother. *Voice of the Old Wolf* deals only peripherally with that war, but the book is a well written biography and a good, well illustrated source on an overlooked period in Nez Perce history.

Encyclopedia of American Indian Wars, 1492-1890, by Jerry Keenan (Santa Barbara: ABC-CLIO, 1997). 278pp. Illus., biblio., d.j. Cloth, $60.00.

Encyclopedia of the War of 1812, edited by David S. Heidler and Jeanne T. Heidler (Santa Barbara: ABC-CLIO, 1997), 636pp. Illus., maps, appendices, chronology, glossary, biblio., index, d.j. Cloth, $99.50.

These two encyclopedias are the first in what will apparently be a series by the ABC-CLIO press (a book on the Spanish-American war is projected). *Indian Wars* is the first general encyclopedia-format reference work on American Indian conflicts. The articles on wars, battles, policies, and leaders range in length from a paragraph to two pages, apparently depending on the significance or notoriety of the events and persons discussed. [For an interview with author Jerry Keenan, see pp. 75-84 in this issue.] The bibliography is lengthy and current and will be useful in seeking further references (although it is heavily weighted with books versus articles). Few totally essential subjects are omitted. However, the book omits biographies of several important individuals of the period of exploration and colonization (Columbus for example), and there are virtually no references to events beyond the boundaries of the U.S. Such omissions may be due to the book's main shortcoming, which is its length. It is mystifying that the press produced a work on the Indian wars, a lengthy and important series of events, less than half as long as its work on the War of 1812. In fact, it appears from the numeral "I" left on the title page that a two volume work was projected and halted. The result is a book that is neither particularly affordable nor definitive. However, the fact that there is no similar book available, and that this one is clearly written and generally accurate, makes it a useful resource for individuals, an essential one for libraries.

War of 1812 is far more comprehensive than *Indian Wars*. The work is a compilation of articles by a variety of authorities. There are a number of maps (notably missing from *Indian Wars*) and appendices of diplomatic and legislative information. *War of 1812*'s particular value to Indian wars readers is the inclusion of a good many Indian battles, including some of the previous conflicts in the "Old Northwest," the Creek (Muskogee) War, and the campaigns of Tecumseh and other pan-Indian leaders.

The book does contain a few errors, most evident when it deals with the continent's European colonial background. For example, New Orleans is mistakenly identified as the first successful European settlement in Louisiana. The books' steep cost ($99.50) will discourage many readers from purchasing it. However, *War of 1812* is a unique and important reference work and should be acquired by libraries.

Chasing Shadows: Apaches and Yaquis Along the United States-Mexico Border, 1876-1911, by Shelly Bowen Hartfield (Albuquerque: University of New Mexico Press, 1998), 200pp. Photos, map, notes, biblio., index, d.j. Cloth, $35.00.

Recently the Yaqui people have been pursuing their claim to cross national borders at will before international tribunals. Ironically, as author Shelly Bowen Hatfield notes, a history of conflict with the Yaqui earlier led to just such an agreement between the Yaquis' enemies, Mexico and the U.S, which permitted one another's troops to cross without formalities when in "hot pursuit" of tribe members. Part of *Chasing Shadows* is good traditional military history, but the book is also one of the few to deal with how commercial development fueled Indian wars and how two different countries pursued different approaches to dealing with Indians. Although both the U.S. and Mexico shared an interest in relocating the Yaqui for the benefit of miners, farmers, and railroad builders, Mexico often resorted to forced labor or scalp bounties, while the U.S. preferred the reservation system and military campaigns. Although generally clearly written, *Chasing Shadows* has a few editing problems, including the frequent omission of commas.

Red Cloud: Warrior-Statesman of the Lakota Sioux, by Robert W. Larson (Norman: University of Oklahoma Press, 1997), 336pp. Illustrations, biblio., index, d.j. Cloth, $24.95.

Autobiography of Red Cloud, War Leader of the Oglalas, edited by R. Eli Paul (Helena: Montana Historical Society Press, 1997), 219pp. Illustrations, map, appendices, notes, index, d.j. Cloth, $27.95; paperback, $15.95.

Few Indian leaders have become as famous, or remained as enigmatic, as the Oglala Sioux chief Red Cloud (Makhpiya-Luta). Known as the only Indian leader to win a war (1866-1867) with the U.S. Army, historians are only now beginning to fully appreciate Red Cloud's skills in non-violent resistance as well. Red Cloud was long regarded by many whites as obstinate and deceptive and by many Indians as defeatist and compliant in later life. Now, however, authors like Robert W. Larson are arguing that Red Cloud was a realist who skillfully managed to win concessions from the U.S. government and to delay the Oglala's cultural assimilation.

Though promotion for Larson's *Red Cloud* states that the book is "imbued with the new social and environmental history," it is largely traditional in approach except for an initial chapter on "Sioux" migration and expansion. Author Larson has used virtually all of the limited sources on Red Cloud to produce an authoritative and judicious biography. The text is densely worded, but its direction is easy to follow. Unfortunately, *Red Cloud* contains no footnotes or endnotes, limiting its value for students and researchers. Despite this drawback, the book deserves a place on the shelves of those wishing to understand the Oglala and other Plains Indians.

The discovery that a manuscript purporting to be a reminiscence by Red Cloud was genuine was a great aid to Larson in producing his biography. The manuscript itself was shortly thereafter published as *Autobiography of Red Cloud*. Its introduction provides an interesting explanation by editor R. Eli Paul of how he deduced that an elderly Red Cloud had dictated the gist of the account to a French Canadian fur trader. *Autobiography* deals with the years before Red Cloud gained celebrity and before his leadership against the Army. The book is of great worth for two reasons. First, it contains a good deal of material on inter-tribal warfare, a subject that non-Indian historians were usually tardy in recording. Second, it is one of the longest authentic accounts of the values and conduct of a young "Sioux" warrior. In addition, like many Montana Historical Society books, *Autobiography of Red Cloud* is attractively priced.

The Apalachee Indians and Mission San Luis, by John H. Hann and Bonnie G. McEwan (Gainesville: University Press of Florida,1998), 193pp. Illustrations, maps, appendix, biblio., index, d.j. Cloth, $49.95.

The Timucuan Chiefdoms of Spanish Florida, Vol. 2: Resistance and Destruction, by John E Worth (Gainesville: University Press of Florida,1998), 274pp. Illus., maps, tables, appendices, notes, biblio., index, d.j. Cloth, $49.95.

Books dealing with eastern, seventeeth century, or non-English Indian conflicts are relatively scare. Those meeting all three criteria are the rarest of all. For this reason, the appearance of *The Apalachee Indians* and *The Timucuan Chiefdoms* is very welcome.

At first glance, the title *The Apalachee Indians and Mission San Luis* would not seem to promise an examination of inter-tribal or white-Indian hostilities. In fact, however, the book contains a surprising amount of material on the Spanish military, the forgotten Apalachee and Timucuan "revolts" against the Spanish, and the devastating impact on the Indians of inter-colonial wars. The Apalachee Indian nation was among the first that the Spanish attempted to assimilate in North America. Mission San Luis, the primary Apalachee mission, was the de facto western capital of Spanish Florida; as such, the community was the object of raids by the English and their Indian allies.

The *Apalachee Indians* is a rarity in more than its subject matter. Its text is so clear and concise that the book can be used and appreciated by anyone from a middle school student to a graduate faculty member. Furthermore, the work is one of the most profusely and beautifully illustrated ever to emerge from an academic press. There are an astounding 120 color maps, reconstructions, photographs, and cutaway views. Such illustrations are one reason that this book is unusually effective in making a "lost" Indian nation real and concrete to readers.

The Timucuan Indians, like their longtime enemies the Apalachee, have been almost forgotten. John E. Worth, using archaeological work and Spanish documents, had done an outstanding job of reconstructing the tribe's history.

The result is volumes 1 and 2 of *The Timucuan Chiefdoms of Spanish Florida*. Whereas *The Apalachee Indians* uses color pictures to recreate the material culture of one Indian nation, *Timucuan Chiefdoms* uses precise narration to reconstruct the military and political events of another. Readers will find that the series of ambushes, murders, and reprisals between the Spanish and the Timucuans makes Indian wars of later centuries, or west of the Mississippi River, seem almost tame by comparison. In the end, the Timucuans were destroyed by the genocidal side effects of the same English-Spanish warfare that annihilated the Apalachee. *Volume 2: Resistance and Destruction* is preceded by *Volume 1: Assimilation*. However, *Volume 1* deals largely with the Spanish colonial and mission systems and will be of far less interest to those seeking information on Indian wars.

Books Received for Review

Reaping the Whirlwind: The Apache Wars, by Peter Aleshire (Facts on File, 1998.)

From Laramie to Wounded Knee: In the West That Was, by Charles W. Allen, Richard E. Jensen, ed. (University of Nebraska Press, 1997.)

Army Museums West of the Mississippi, by Fred. L. Bell (Hellgate Press, 1997).

Whitney Gallery of Western Art, by Sarah E. Boehme (Buffalo Bill Historical Center, 1997.)

American Indians in World War I, At War and At Home, by Thomas A. Britten (University of New Mexico Press, 1997.)

Cheyennes at Dark Water Creek: The Last Fight of the Red River War, by William Y. Chalfont (University of Oklahoma Press, 1997.)

The Massacre at Wounded Knee: Narrative Voices, by Bruce Cutler (University of Oklahoma Press, 1995. Paperback edition, 1997.)

Rethinking American Indian History, edited by Donald L. Fixico (University of New Mexico Press, 1997.)

Firearms of the American West, 1866-1894, by Louis A. Garavaglia and Charles G. Worman (University Press of Colorado, 1985, 1997.)

A Face in the Rock: The Tale of a Grand Island Chippewa, by Loren R. Graham (University of California Press, 1995. Paperback edition, 1998.)

McIntosh and Weatherford, Creek Indian Leaders, by Benjamin W. Griffith, Jr. (University of Alabama Press, 1998.)

The Navajos in 1705: Roque Madrid's Campaign Journal, edited by Rick Hendricks and John P. Wilson (University of New Mexico Press, 1996).

Two-Spirit People: Native American Gender Identity, Sexuality, and Spirituality, edited by Sue-Ellen Jacobs, Wesley Thomas, and Sabine Lang (University of Illinois Press,1997.)

American Indian Activism: Alcatraz to the Longest Walk, T. Johnson, J. Nagel, and D. Champagne, eds. (University of Chicago Press, 1997.)

The Powder River Expedition Journals of Colonel Richard Irving Dodge, edited by Wayne R. Kime (University of Oklahoma, 1997).

The Pueblo Revolt of 1680, by Andrew L. Knaut (Norman: University of Oklahoma Press, 1995. Paperback edition, 1997.)

Indian Wars in North Carolina, 1663-1763, by E. Lawrence Lee (Division of Archives and History, 1963. Reprint, 1997.)

Warriors of the Plains, by Thomas E. Mails (Council Oak Books, 1997.)

Roadside History of Nebraska, by Candy Moulton (Mountain Press Publishing Company, 1997.)

Indians in the United States and Canada: A Comparative History, by Roger L. Nichols (University of Nebraska Press, 1998).

Lakota Noon: The Indian Narrative of Custer's Defeat, by Gregory F. Michno (Mountain Press Publishing Company, 1997).

The Nebraska Indian Wars Reader, 1865-1877, edited by R. Eli Paul (University of Nebraska Press, 1998).

Black Valor: Buffalo Soldiers and the Medal of Honor, by Frank N. Schubert (Scholarly Resources, 1997.)

Tecumseh and the Shawnee Confederation, by Rebecca Stefoff (Facts on File, 1998.)

Tecumseh: A Life, by John Sugden (Henry Holt and Company, 1997.)

Making Peace with Cochise: The 1872 Journal of Captain Joseph Alton Sladen, Edwin R. Sweeney, ed. (University of Oklahoma Press, 1997.)

Custer and the Great Controversy: The Origin and Development of a Legend, by Robert M. Utley (University of Nebraska Press, 1962. Paperback edition, 1998.)

Roadside History of Florida, by Douglas Waitley (Missoula: Mountain Press Publishing Company, 1997).

Frontier Soldier: An Enlisted Man's Journal of the Sioux and Nez Perce Campaigns, 1877, by William Frederick Zimmer and Jerome A. Greene (Helena: Montana Historical Society Press, 1998.)

Index

NEW AND FORTHCOMING TITLES FROM SAVAS PUBLISHING COMPANY!

1876 Facts About Custer and the Battle of the Little Bighorn,
Jerry Russell

Custer's defeat comes alive in this entertaining book, the third in our "Facts About" history series! Russell (the founder of the Order of the Indian Wars), breaks down and sets forth the campaigns facts, anecdotes, myths, and legends. This handy reference guide offers several categories for each side, and will please everyone from the general reader to the serious scholar. A superb addition to the Little Bighorn bookshelf. ISBN 1-882810-34-1. Map, drawings, photos, bibliography. Paper. 240pp. JUNE. $11.95

1836 Facts About the Alamo and the Texas War For Independence,
Mary Deborah Petite

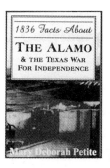

The second book in our popular "Facts About" history series. This fresh presentation delves into the lives and experiences of the people swept up by the war, with a focus on the fatal last stand. Presented in an original and entertaining style, with in-depth information on every man who fought in the Alamo. Also includes coverage of the war's battles and engagements, myths and legends, naval affairs, weapons, an examination of both armies' organizations, and biographies of every leading officer. ISBN 1-882810-35-X. Map, drawings, photos, bibliography. Paper. 192pp. $11.95

The Generals of Gettysburg:
The Leaders of America's Greatest Battle
Larry Tagg

An encyclopedia of every brigade level (or higher) officer, including colonels, who served at Gettysburg. Includes a photo of each man with in-depth information on educational background, career experiences, physical and emotional attributes, and a full discussion of his military experience up to the Gettysburg Campaign; Comprehensive treatment of what each officer did at Gettysburg, and a summation of his post-Gettysburg career and a suggested reading list. "Indispensible!" ISBN 1-882810-30-9, 9 maps, 148 photos, biographical reading list, cloth, d.j., 374pp. $29.95

- FREE CATALOG AVAILABLE UPON REQUEST -

Savas Publishing Company
202 First Street S.E., Suite 103A, Mason City, IA 50401
515-421-7135 (editorial offices, catalogs, and inquiries)

Distributed by Stackpole Books, 5067 Ritter Road, Mechancisburg, PA 17055 (Orders: 1-800-732-3669)